D1488788

Cathedrals Now

Their use and place in society

ESSAYS BY
Robert Jeffery
David Shearlock
Richard Lewis
Hugh Dickinson
John Moses
John Arnold

Edited by

Iain M. MacKenzie

The Canterbury Press
Norwich

© The Contributors 1996

First published 1996 by The Canterbury Press Norwich
(a publishing imprint of Hymns Ancient & Modern Limited,
a registered charity)
St Mary's Works, St Mary's Plain,
Norwich, Norfolk, NR3 3BH

British Library Cataloguing in Publication Date

A catalogue record for this book is available
from the British Library

ISBN 1–85311–143–0

Typeset, printed and bound in Great Britain by
The Lavenham Press Ltd
Lavenham, Suffolk

CONTENTS

FOREWORD

The English Cathedral confronts many people as a mystery. Some (and even those knowledgeable on most church matters) perceive them as anachronisms; others as institutions ripe for radical reform; yet others as museums housing the relics of the past and, as such, tourist attractions. The critics include those who airily dismiss the building of Cathedrals as a statement in stone and art of human arrogance and pretentiousness. In fact, Cathedrals mean different things to different people – even those who staff them and spend their days ministering in them and from them, maintaining them, and generally ordering their continuance.

A dispassionate look at Cathedrals, however, would reveal much. The visitor should be aware that even in the most inaccessible places in medieval Cathedrals, the craftsmen were as careful of their skills as they were of the parts of the building immediate to the sight. That all work, even that not normally seen by human eye, was offered *ad maiorem gloriam Dei, to the greater glory of God*, can be instanced from this alone. Whatever element of human pride and unworthy motive may have crept in, the motivation of the vision of offering human endeavour, exercise of all art, and above all – for to this all else was directed – the worship of God, was, and is, paramount. Music, architecture, sculpture, carving, painting, education, hospitality and welcome, were all, and still are, circled round prayer and praise and proclamation as their servants. And still, so much behind the scenes in all these areas of Cathedral life, is, like the work of the builders of old, unseen and sometimes unappreciated by the casual observer and visitor.

It is sometimes also supposed that those who hold Cathedral appointments are the recipients of sinecures. No doubt in days gone by, in certain periods of history, there was substance to such a conclusion. But generally, and certainly not today, this is far from the case. Gone are the days when Deans and Canons Residentiary merely fulfilled the minimum of duties or their few months of residence and mingled them with their profitable pluralities. The chapters of this book which follow will give an idea of the busy-ness of Cathedral life in all its aspects, and, it is hoped, will bring an appreciation of the often unseen demands made on all who work within and for that life, and the dedication of so many to it.

It is also hoped that in a time when Cathedrals are under scrutiny, not least in the recommendations of the Archbishops' Commission on Cathedrals Report to be debated by the Church, these chapters will be informative to the wider Church and the general public, clearing up misconceptions and leading to a deeper appreciation of a most important part of our Christian heritage and of what is offered by Cathedrals for the propagation and upholding of the Gospel of Christ to this land in their diocesan and national roles and responsibilities.

So often, Cathedrals are in the vanguard of the proclamation of that Gospel, for many a tourist visiting them, with sensitive welcoming to what should be manifestly seen to be a house of pilgrimage and prayer and worship, may have his or her first introduction to what Christianity is all about. This is an awesome responsibility.

In truth, while there are 'categories' of Cathedrals (those on the 'Old Foundation', those on the 'New Foundation' and Parish Church Cathedrals), all Cathedrals are different. Their respective histories, the way in which they have been perceived in the past, the clergy who have served them throughout the generations, their geographical placing, the patronage they have enjoyed (or rued!) – all have contributed to their respective individualities. Each is a treasure in its own right, but, with its own particular contribution, part of that higher vision common to all Christian people, of serving God with heart and mind, hand and voice, to the best of our ability.

A foreword is no place for adding yet more views on the matter in hand. The views set out in all that follows are the result of much thought and care by Deans and Provosts. These chapters are commended to the widest possible public, and, it is also hoped, to the thoughts and prayers and appreciation of the reader for the part of the Church's life expressed in the witness and work of the Cathedral Churches of this land.

The chapters themselves are, in substance, lectures delivered at the annual series in St Giles-in-the-Fields, London WC2. As Registrar of these lectures I am grateful to the Deans and Provosts represented in this book, who most graciously made time in the midst of extremely busy lives, to deliver the lectures and to be involved in all the writing up necessary before publication. Gratitude is also due to the Revd Gordon Taylor, the Rector of St Giles-in-the-Fields, whose insight in setting up the series of lectures every year since 1971, (at which there have been, to date, just over 30,000 attendances), has given a wide and stable platform for Christian education.

Thanks are also due to Mr Kenneth Baker and the staff of The Canterbury Press Norwich, whose unfailing courtesy and helpfulness have facilitated my task of co-ordinating this publication.

IAIN M. MACKENZIE
Canon Residentiary of Worcester

1

Cathedrals - Mission in Reverse

ROBERT JEFFERY
The Dean of Worcester

'I firmly believe in One Holy Catholic and Apostolic Church,' said Archbishop William Temple, 'and I sincerely regret that it does not exist.' It is easy to see what he meant. The vision of the church is of people set apart, preaching a gospel of universal application, united one with another and going out to bring the peace of God to all people. That is the Vision. The reality is far from it. We are a divided church, we sometimes seem so trapped in the culture of our age that it is hard to see the holiness; our expression of the faith is often limited to certain classes and cultures in society and we show a strange reluctance to be sent out in mission.

This tension between the Vision and the reality can also be seen in the history of our cathedrals. Here the biggest temptation is introversion – a refusal of mission and a self-centredness which is a denial of the Christian life. Established as centres of diocesan life, they became so corrupt that people like Dunstan and Oswald saw hope for them only by turning them into monastic institutions. In this capacity cathedrals became centres of learning, piety and pilgrimage and as powerful landlords they began to meet their own needs rather than the world around them. The Reformation wrought another change. The monastic mould in some cathedrals was replaced by a corporate and collegiate model and yet by the end of the eighteenth century they were again places for an enclosed élite. Cathedrals were both locked and neglected and you had to bribe a verger to get in. The Victorians gave much thought and consideration to the role of cathedrals and changes were made which both removed many of their assets (for the sake or urban mission) and forced them to engage more fully with the wider world. Cathedral appeals and restoration programmes forced some new thinking. The Victorian restoration of cathedrals and the development of new dioceses helped to turn them outwards, but the temptation is ever present for cathedrals to turn in on themselves. A blinkered attitude to the world comes over many in cathedral communities. They often cannot see beyond their own awesome needs and responsibilities. Some talk of a demonic in cathedral life, the folk memory and myth which prevents change, flexibility and openness towards the world around. It is only too easy in cathedral life to feed on the very rich inheritance and become bloated and puffed up in one's own tradition. It is far easier to collude with people who dislike change than to challenge and resist an introverted life. The very need to maintain the fabric of the vast buildings encourages an introverted mentality. There is very often a dark side to cathedral life and it has to be named and acknowledged. The advent of the tourist trade has led to a further dimension. For we can so easily see tourists as a source of income and nothing else. We can be so blinkered by our needs for money that we end up by exploiting people just like others in the tourist trade.

But before pursuing this further we need to define our terms and consider the role and function of Mission in the life of the Church. The word 'Apostolic' in the creed sums it up. An apostle is someone who is sent and the basis of mission lies in the fact that God is a sending God. The basic text for mission is in the words of the Risen Christ in St John's Gospel (chapter 20 verse 21):

> Peace be with you. As my father has sent me even so send I you.

What Jesus comes to bring is PEACE/SHALOM/WHOLE-NESS/HOLINESS. These are the deeper meanings of the word salvation. There is in it that harmony and well-being and wholeness of relationships which lie at the heart of the word SHALOM. The Risen Christ is sent to unite us with himself in the same way as he is united with God. That lies at the heart of Johannine theology. That is what the mission is to achieve.

God is a sending God; he sends prophets, he sends leaders, he sends agents like Cyrus, King of Persia, to bring his people to their senses. Jesus also sends out his disciples to preach and announce the Kingdom. There is a continuous process of movement. The early missions in Britain were also that of movement. The cathedrals in this context were some of the earliest bases of Mission. The religious communities of the Minsters were centres from which people went out to preach and establish Christian communities. The great St Wulfstan of Worcester perpetually travelled, prayed in churches, built churches, preached in the open air, denounced wickedness, including slavery. The cathedral was the centre from which mission emerged.

But today the scene is very different. Hence my title 'Mission in Reverse'. Since the advent of Tourism cathedrals do not have to go out; people pour into them. Thus the mission is to those who come in rather than to those to whom we are sent out. This poses a particular opportunity and a challenge to cathedrals and this is the matter which I wish to address.

Over the years various models of mission have been propounded. The most recent and popular exposition of this has been the Publication from the General Synod entitled *The Measure of Mission*. This expounded what were called 'The Ten marks of mission' which was to help enable people to assess how far they were sharing in mission. They expressed those attitudes in the gospel which enable us to enter into God's shalom.

But more important for our purpose, to begin with, is to look at models of mission to which cathedrals may relate.

MISSION AS PRESENCE. All mission begins with presence. Great churches and cathedrals by their very presence point to God. Thus by their inner and community life they affirm the presence of God. It is deeply moving to attend the Daily Office in a cathedral when you realise that these acts of worship, or variations of them, have been sung or said in that place without a break from the sixth or seventh century. This tradition is mission in its own right. The daily offering of worship and the manner of worship needs to be very carefully thought out, and consideration given to its power to speak of God in that particular place. Thus it is important to known of old customs, of long-standing traditions. The very design of a building speaks of worship and needs to be respected to get worship right. Worship in a cathedral is big theatre and has to be treated as such, but so we affirm God's presence. This in itself poses interesting mission questions. It was Professor J. G. Davies in his important book *Worship and Mission* who called for worship itself to have a missionary element. The words used in worship should be understandable, the concepts graspable. Much cathedral worship has a 'contemplative' feel to it. This can communicate a great deal of the mystery and wonder of God. So at its heart the mission of a cathedral is centred in prayer and worship and a community which shares in it. Without that all is lost.

MISSION AS TRANSLATION. If the scriptures had not been translated we would not understand them. Thus an essential tool of mission as translation is from one area of concept to another. A cathedral needs to be a place of interpretation of this at several levels:

Historical. Cathedrals are wonderful places to demonstrate how God acts in history. Through the building, its monuments, its stories, you can trace the history of the nation, and beyond. Worcester with King John, Prince Arthur and the scene of the battle of Worcester can show many aspects of English life. But the story needs telling, people need to be shown how the sacred and the secular are tied together and how God works in all.

Doctrine. As a building for Christian worship a cathedral is full of Christian symbols, from simple things like the pulpit, font, altars, and crosses, to more complex imagery in tapestry, windows and murals. In our very secular age these need interpretation so that people can understand. Guides and welcomers need training to use opportunities to talk through the meaning of Christian symbols.

Teaching. The cathedral as the seat of the Bishop and a place of teaching can have a wide role in education and learning and encouraging the knowledge of the Christian faith. This is becoming ever more important as the role is being given up by universities and others who are now required to give people accreditations. Many do not want this; they just want knowledge to work on and chew over. So a cathedral can help to broaden the mind and strengthen the heart.

MISSION AS DIALOGUE. The very fact that cathedrals are centres of tourism make them into places of dialogue with people of all faiths and none. What do the vast number of Japanese tourists make of our buildings? Some cathedrals situated in areas of immigrant communities will find a strong request not only for dialogue but to be used for worship. I believe dialogue must come before worship. But could parts of cathedrals, like Chapter Houses, be used for worship by other faiths and so engender tolerance and community?

But the dialogue is with many others. The major planning of a civic service; the newspaper editor who wants a carol service for his staff; the TA officer planning Remembrance Sunday; the retired schoolmistress organising a charitable concert: everyone of these is open to dialogue about what they want in a service and why; how the liturgy can reflect the life from which it comes. There are opportunities to probe and question people's assumptions and to look deeply into issues. So we see here a mission not just to individuals but to social structures and organisations which affect the life of people. A mission which neglects structures is only partial.

MISSION AS CONTEXTUALISATION. Much is written and thought about how the gospel may be made relevant in differing cultures, for example Bede Griffiths. This may be through liturgy and experimental patterns of worship, eg. rock music, raves in the nave, etc., but it may equally be a sensitivity to the situation in which a cathedral is placed or the community it lives among and can engage with it. Risks of culture traps are always there, by which I mean being so trapped in the contemporary culture that the Gospel cannot be seen. Nevertheless in serving the community a cathedral relates to its context. Its history and life contribute a great deal to the cultural environment.

MISSION AS THE QUEST FOR JUSTICE. Just because the cathedral stands where it is, it has the opportunity to challenge accepted standards, to make people think, to provoke new thought. A Tourism exhibition was held at Worcester which looked at the ethics of the tourist trade and pointed to its misuse in child prostitution in Asia and other problems. It caused great offence, but it made people think. One Holy Week we had a Stations of the Cross based on pictures from Auschwitz, which moved people deeply. In the crypt we have a contemporary Pietà by Glynn Williams which draws attention to the suffering of humanity. Cathedrals draw many strange people; the drug addict, the tramp, the mentally disturbed, and such encounters raise questions of justice and often are opportunities to examine the big issues in society.

MISSION AS EVANGELISM. Communicating the faith is not just verbal. These great buildings have a power to communicate in their own right. This was well expressed by Archbishop John Habgood in a sermon at Worcester in 1984 entitled 'Significant Space':

> I speak of generosity of spirit... not only because all of us need it, but because cathedrals at their best have represented it. Here to this place anyone may come in faith or unfaith, here through liturgy, through art, through music, through architec-

ture, the eternal truths of God are offered to all those who have eyes to see and ears to hear and spirits to respond. Here in this place saints and sinners have jostled and jostle still. Here God can touch us, and heal us and transform us as he touched, healed and transformed countless people before us. Here he can take us our of ourselves, out of the hand of the enemy and set our feet in a large room.

This is a fine description of evangelism. It is not just words but it can be words. It may often be listening; we have trained our welcomers in the art of listening. Conversion is not something we do, it is something God does; but our own attitude can either help or hinder. It has been a popular adage that the task of cathedrals is to turn tourists into pilgrims. A visit to a cathedral is an invitation to pilgrimage and we can be more articulate about that, showing people what a pilgrim was and could be. There need to be places of quiet for prayer, space for people to be, opportunities for people to be taken out of themselves. That is the great opportunity which cathedrals have.

But deeper than any model of mission is the attitude which is open to the world, open to people, open to God. Fr Bernard Haring expresses it well in the words, 'The doors to mental health swing outwards'. Our task is to be open to all.

In 1958 the poet Clive Sansom published a book of poetry entitled *The Cathedral*. In writing the poems he drew on aspects of Cathedral life in England. Near the end is a poem entitled:

PRAYER

We pray thee, Spirit of God, that our spirits,
Rising like these arches towards heaven,
Grant us, through windows of imagination, a glimpse
To which we shall return. Buttress our belief,
Within this world of time, in that world's values;
Let us feel, within the play of stresses,
The beauty, goodness, truth, survive destruction
Of earthly counterparts, and in thy kingdom
Will stand eternally. Open our doors,
O spirit of love, to thy spirit; make us one

With thy creating hand, spirit of life –
That we may be, and know ourselves to be,
A brick, a stone, within thy vast design.

The mission is God's mission, not ours, but we all have our part. An open cathedral, in the hearts and minds of those who serve it, can indeed be mission in reverse. For Cathedrals draw us out of ourselves. If we can avoid the risks, of introversion we have a major part to play in God's total mission to the world.

'As my father has sent me even so send I you.'

2

Cathedrals and the Christian Musical Tradition

DAVID SHEARLOCK
The Dean of Truro

I would like to begin by asking you to listen very carefully for ten seconds ...

Well, the **good** news is that you are not going deaf. The **bad** news is that we are unable to fill that silence with the sound of a cathedral organ and a cathedral choir, for no amount of words can ever be an adequate substitute for some real examples of my theme.

Were this a **service**, we would perhaps begin with an Introit: incidentally, 'Introit' is a Cornishman's way of telling you that something is wrong. And were this a **sermon**, my text from Scripture would probably come from Psalm 98, in a version which would not easily be recognised by those of you fortunate enough to subsist on a diet of Miles Coverdale:

> Break into songs of joy, sing psalms in the Lord's honour, with the lyre and with resounding music, with trumpets and echoing horn.

For those of you who are organists, please read *Gamba* for lyre, *8' Tuba* for trumpet, and *Cornopean* for echoing horn. Or maybe I would turn to Ephesians, chapter 5, for those splendid words of Saint Paul:

Sing and make music from your heart to the Lord.

Or, even better, those other words of Saint Paul (1 Corinthians 14.15), which form the motto of the Royal School of Church Music: *Psallam spiritu et mente:*

I will sing with the spirit and with the understanding also.

However, this is not a sermon, and yet I would want **all** those words of Scripture to find an echo in much of what I am going to say, because one of the things which makes a cathedral different from nearly all other churches is its music, music performed above all to the glory of God, and music which draws a large part of its inspiration from the Bible.

It is often said that a cathedral is a symbol, a sign of God's presence in the world of everyday, its towers and spires pointing us in the direction of heaven; its vast open spaces telling us of the vastness of God's glory and God's love; its welcome to all comers a sign of the unity which is inherent in the Trinity of three persons and one God.

Furthermore, the Dean and Chapter will always be wise to remember that the cathedral is the Bishop's church, situated at the spiritual (if not the geographical) centre of the diocese, where a team of clergy and lay people exist primarily to maintain the daily round of worship, with the regular heartbeat of the daily office of Morning and Evening Prayer (Matins and Evensong) and the Eucharist, as the sign of Christ's real presence among his people. Every other aspect of the incredibly varied life of a cathedral has, or should have, its roots in this.

Whether or not there is music at a service, the cathedral and its clergy are there to proclaim the Gospel of Jesus Christ, and woe betide them if they ever forget this or, worse still, if they allow the cathedral's music to become an end in itself, rather than a part, albeit a glorious part, of that proclamation.

So I do not intend to offer you a detailed argument for the importance of the Christian musical tradition, though I would want that importance to extend from the cathedral outwards to the churches and chapels of the diocese. However, I do **not** mean that the latter should try to ape the former, especially as the musical gap between the two appears to be ever-widening. What I **do** mean is that the cathedral should exploit all the advantages it already possesses by virtue of its unique history and unrivalled resources, in order to set and maintain a standard of excellence (and I am well aware that 'excellence' is not a politically correct word in certain circles), a standard which serves as exemplar, though not one to be slavishly imitated.

Ideally, too, the cathedral organist and choir will act as ambassadors, both within the diocese and further afield. Truro Cathedral choir, for example, has recently given a recital in the parish church of Launceston and sung the main Sunday mass in the Cathedral of Notre Dame, in Paris.

* * *

Let us, then, turn to look at the 'Christian Musical Tradition', *Christian*, you will note, and not just Anglican, or even English, for much of the repertoire of our cathedrals is drawn from the Roman Catholic tradition and from the continental Protestant tradition. What, alas, we simply cannot do at this time is to consider in detail the wonderful **history** of that tradition. There is a great deal of literature available on the subject and some splendid biographies of many of its leading figures. As the writer of the Epistle to the Hebrews might have put it, time would fail me to tell of Dunstable, Byrd, Gibbons, Purcell, Attwood, S.S. Wesley, Parry, Howells, Tippett and Shephard.

Something of the tradition lingers on from the magic era of Barchester: indeed, I can assure you that Barchester is still alive and well in some of our cathedrals today! Here is a brief extract from the writings of Trollope (Anthony, you will understand, not Joanna):

> The service was certainly well performed. Such was always the case at Barchester, as the musical education of the choir had been good, and the voices had been carefully selected. The

psalms were beautifully chanted, the Te Deum was magnificently sung; and the litany was given in a manner, which is still to be found at Barchester, but if my taste be correct, is to be found nowhere else. The litany in Barchester Cathedral has long been the special task to which Mr. Harding's skill and voice have been devoted. Crowded audiences generally make good performers, and though Mr. Harding was not aware of any extraordinary exertion on his part, yet probably he rather exceeded his usual mark. Others were doing their best, and it was natural that he should emulate his brethren.

Over two centuries before Trollope's Barchester, John Milton, himself an accomplished musician, wrote a poem in which he celebrates the pleasures of solitude and quietness, in which to reflect on music. Composed in 1632, *Il Penseroso*, and that must surely be a misprint for *Il Penserioso* (the Contemplative), contains these lines:

> But let my due feet never fail
> To walk the studious cloisters pale,
> And love the high embowed roof,
> With antique pillars massy proof,
> And storied windows richly dight,
> Casting a dim religious light.
> There let the pealing organ blow
> To the full-voiced choir below,
> In service high, and anthems clear,
> As may with sweetness, through my ear,
> Dissolve me into ecstasies,
> And bring all heaven before mine eyes.

The same poet, John Milton, has actually provided the title for a very important document, called *In Tune with Heaven*, published as the report of the Archbishops' Commission on Church Music. In his ode 'At a Solemn Music', which I would guess is better known to many of us in the guise of Parry's anthem, *Blest Pair of Sirens*, we find these resonant words:

> O may we soon again renew that song,
> And keep in tune with heaven, till God ere long

To his celestial consort us unite,
To live with him, and sing in endless morn of light.

However, we need to be realistic about all this, and perhaps issue a spiritual health warning to the effect that not all churchgoers are turned on by music. Indeed, not all music lovers are turned on by religion!

Just over a decade ago, that eminent Dean of Salisbury, Sydney Evans, wrote an article for the Friends of Cathedral Music. Here is a brief extract:

> There are those whose presence at choral services would seem to be motivated more by aesthetic than by religious considerations. But who can distinguish the aesthetic from the spiritual, beauty from goodness, art from usefulness, worship from life? 'Signals of transcendence' are what they are for those who can read them as such. Not all Christians, nor all seekers after truth, would find with Herbert that 'heaven upon earth' at choral evensong. Music can, I suppose, become a substitute for God.

That is a danger of which all cathedral musicians need to be aware, Deans and Chapters, Provosts and Councils, Organists and Precentors, Lay Clerks and Choristers. Yet if the music does actually succeed in lifting the soul of humanity into the nearer presence of God, it is serving as a vehicle of redemption, a means of grace, and for that one cannot but be profoundly thankful.

Later I will be pointing in the direction of what I perceive to be some of the threats to the choral tradition, but first I would like to address some of the other problems which face cathedrals today. Some of them are inherent in the system, others are more specific to the conditions of contemporary cathedral and church life. Some are financial problems, but the majority are to do with people, so let me say, and let me say it loudly and clearly, that the Church as a whole is enormously in debt to its musicians, and obviously in this context I mean particularly those who serve in our cathedrals.

I have nothing but intense admiration for the skill and devotion of organists (by whatever title they happen to be known), of lay clerks (ditto) and of choristers, not to mention the wives and parents of those involved, many of whom make immense sacrifices of money, time, energy and family life, in order to keep the tradition going.

The choristers themselves, mainly aged between 7 and 13 are (may I put it this way?) the unsung heroes (and heroines) of our story, whether they be boarders in a choir school, day boys rounded up from the local community, or something in between, such as our boys at Truro, all of whom are educated at a local preparatory school, Polwhele House, largely at the expense of the Dean and Chapter, and who come in daily from places as far apart as Falmouth and Newquay, St Ives and St Austell.

Recruitment is clearly one of the major problems in many cathedrals, though it never ceases to amaze me, in today's social and educational climate, that so many boys come forward every year to fill nearly all the available places in our cathedrals and college chapel choirs. The calibre of these boys is astonishing: as well as having to cope with all the other demands of school, domestic and social life, they have all the weight of their choir commitments and will almost certainly be having tuition in at least one musical instrument. No wonder so many of them end up as professional musicians.

And what about the girls, you will be saying? Well, the initiative of Richard Seal of Salisbury Cathedral, boldly to go beyond the traditional frontiers by having a girls' choir in a cathedral, has now been copied in a number of places. The success of this venture lies, it seems to me, in not putting the girls in with the boys (though Manchester is about to do just that), but in having a parallel choir, sometimes singing on their own, sometimes with the men. 'Peaceable co-existence should be the aim', says Harry Bramma, the Director of the Royal School of Church Music.

Heritage and Renewal, the report of the Archbishops' Commission on Cathedrals, actually says nothing startling about music, but does recommend that 'cathedrals should seek to provide chorister education for girls as well as boys'. What I suspect few people want to see is a corresponding reduction in the number of boys in our choirs. There has been an awful lot of prejudice aired in this debate, but we ought not to lose sight of the fact that much of our finest music was written for trebles, not sopranos. It is worth remembering, too, that many clergy have arrived where they are because they were once choristers themselves.

That was certainly the case for me, when I joined the choir at that tender age of innocence when one believed that Quinquagesima was the Sunday when you filled up your fountain pen, and left it when I was just old enough to know that 'rallentando' was a musical sign which prompted you to look up just in case a conductor happened to be present. As the famous 'C.J.' would have said in *The Fall and Rise of Reginald Perrin*, 'I didn't get where I am today without having been a choirboy'. I have since discovered that two and a half choristers in every 100 are later ordained: little did I realise at the time that I was facing odds of 40 to 1!

In all this talk about boys, I am not arguing **against** girls: far from it. But I do want to press the argument in favour of boys, as well, for many of them will be in the back rows of our cathedral choirs in the years to come, just as no doubt some of the girls who are now joining cathedral choirs will one day discover there the beginning of a call to that priesthood which now lies open to them. Some choirs experience more of a problem with getting **men** than they do with boys and girls. Chapel choirs at our universities are obviously in a strong position here, as are those cathedrals which are set in large cities with major educational institutions in and around them, so please spare a thought and a prayer for those less favourably situated, in what are virtually market towns with musically unpromising hinterlands. Yet the maintenance of the musical tradition depends substantially on there being a steady supply of counter tenors or altos, tenors and basses, who can learn music quickly, sing it well, do it for very modest financial rewards and be willing to put in some pretty unsocial hours.

As far as organists are concerned, the reverse problem prevails, in that there are too many well-equipped people in pursuit of too few jobs. There is an unofficial ladder of promotion, whereby one starts as an organ scholar, moves on to become an assistant or sub-organist, takes over a 'starter' cathedral, progresses to a major cathedral, and finally lands up at the console of Canterbury or Westminster, St Paul's or York Minster. Sadly, though, there is a wastage at every stage, as excellent organists simply cannot find suitable posts, and may well drop out of the cathedral tradition altogether.

Let it be remembered, though, that the Cathedral Organist, or Director of Music as he is now increasingly being called, is the lynch-pin of the entire set-up. Almost everything depends on him and this has been more and more recognised by the quality of the remuneration package now on offer, even though it still falls well below the ideal, and well below what the best of them could achieve on the recital circuit. So we should be very careful not to take them for granted and particularly so if they are themselves aware that what they are doing is the fulfilment of a genuine vocation from God.

* * *

Few, if any, cathedrals are not faced with the perennial problem of financing their whole musical enterprise, and we are talking here of very considerable sums of money. It often comes as a surprise, even to people whose lives revolve around cathedrals, to learn that the annual music bill in most of them comes into the 6-figure category. As an example, even a relatively small cathedral such as Truro, which the Football Association would once have described as being in the Third Division (South), spends over £100,000 a year on its music, by which I mean the salaries of the organist and his assistant, the honoraria of the lay vicars, three-quarters of the cost of the school fees of the sixteen choristers, and the provision of music copies, to say nothing of the maintenance of the musical instruments themselves, two organs and three pianos.

A recent survey for the Archbishops' Commission on Cathedrals has shown that, on average, about 12% of a cathedral's expenditure goes on music, with St Paul's ahead at the top of the league, and Truro, incidentally, almost exactly in the middle.

Let me spell that out a little more clearly: for every £8 that a cathedral spends – and remember the massive cost of the maintenance of the fabric alone – £1 will go on music. Perhaps this accounts, at least in part, for the fact that few cathedrals nowadays are able to commission new music from the many contemporary composers who might in another day have looked to the Church for patronage.

Cathedral music is funded from many sources, including current income, trust money, special appeals, endowment funds and (increasingly today) commercial sponsorship. We have no idea how this last one will develop, especially at a time when industry and commerce have been going through a sticky patch, but I imagine that no one in any cathedral in this country is anxious to have logos on choristers' surplices to advertise the detergents in which they are washed or the power source which drives the washing machine. How far, though, do we preserve our aesthetic integrity in the face of mounting difficulties in meeting the bills? Is there a stage at which we have, regretfully, to compromise our valued high standards in order to keep the product alive? These may seem academic questions, with clear-cut answers, to those not directly involved: to others, though, they are becoming ever more pertinent.

*   *   *

I said earlier that I would address some of the matters which, from one perspective or another might be regarded as threats to the cathedral musical tradition. I have already touched on one of them, namely the financial problem: another one, paradoxically, is a musical one, which can be expressed in the form of a question, the answer to which you may care to work out for yourselves. The question is this: should cathedral authorities allow **any** music to be performed, regardless either of its provenance or of the words associated with it? Should those authorities be totally scrupulous in vetting

every single item of every proposed concert or recital programme and allow only those which have impeccably Christian credentials to be put on?

Yes, I am expressing the problem in rather an extreme
form, but answers do not easily come where the issues are not
starkly clear, one way or the other, and I have to say that my
experience so far suggests that the issues seldom present
themselves conveniently in black and white terms. There is,
for instance, a lot of excellent modern music, which clearly
commends itself to a production in the City Hall but which
may not be right in the Cathedral, right, that is, on religious,
as opposed to aesthetic, grounds. On a slightly different level,
what place should be given in a cathedral service to some of
our contemporary hymns and choruses, the musical and spiritual content of which may be ineffably sub-standard?

There is nothing new about this: we all sing some
appallingly badly-written Victorian hymns to some amaz-
ingly banal tunes. Thirty-five years ago, Erik Routley, in his
book *Church Music and Theology*, wrote of 'the persistent
generosity with which the church has for many generations
now offered hospitality to the second rate'.

A more recent, and equally amusing, example is something that was told to me by Lionel Dakers, the former Director of the RSCM and himself a onetime cathedral organist.
He had attended one of those services at which an overhead
projector is an obligatory part of the liturgical provision. On
it flashed the words of the next hymn:

> Jesus, Jesus, Jesus, Jesus,
> Jesus, Jesus, Jesus, Jesus,
> Jesus, Jesus, Jesus, Jesus,
> Jesus, Jesus, Jesus, Jesus,
> to be sung three times
> (words copyright).

That leads me to the next potential threat to the cathedral music tradition and it, also, is a paradoxical one: I refer
to the liturgy. Settings of the Latin Mass and of the Prayer
Book canticles and Communion service are a major compo-

nent of that tradition. Take that away, and you are substantially impoverished. If you are into cathedral music yourself, you will be able to name dozens of examples, ranging from Palestrina's *Missa Brevis* to *Darke in F*, from Byrd's *Great Service* to Walton's *Chichester Service*. But how many really good settings do you know of the ASB Nicene Creed or the Te Deum from Matins? I am not in any way knocking *The Alternative Service Book 1980*, least of all its eucharistic liturgy: I am simply making the point that the best of today's composers are either ignoring it or cannot adequately cope with it.

You may be tempted to think that cathedrals can remain isolated from current trends in liturgy and music. Perhaps they can, for a while, but what is now happening in many parish churches will inevitably find its way into some of our cathedrals in the next decade or two, (a) because more members of existing Chapters resent the financial drain of the traditional music and musicians, and (b) because the next generation of Deans, Provosts and Residentiary Canons is even now being brought up on a very different diet from those of the past or present.

So the influence of the liturgical movement is penetrating even into our cathedrals and there is now to be seen, in some of them, a gradual widening of congregational participation, in the spoken word as well as in music. Whereas, once upon a time, the people were allowed only to sing in the hymns – and then perhaps, a trifle grudgingly – now you may find them involved in Gélineau and Taizé style chants or choruses, in songs of renewal, and even in eucharistic settings. Some cathedrals have also been very successful in their re-ordering of liturgical space: the larger ones find it much more difficult, almost impossible if there is a huge choir screen. In those which have experimented with alternative musical accompaniment, there has always been the recognition that you cannot cut out the organ altogether.

So I reiterate the danger that a cathedral could become indistinguishable from any other church if it fails to exploit properly one of the few things that makes it essentially different, namely its capacity for musical excellence, which to my mind is one of the fundamentals of that tradition which we are considering.

If cathedral music has any kind of 'flagship', I suppose it would have to be Choral Evensong, and that for three reasons: first, because that is what is being done nearly every day in most of our cathedrals; secondly, because that is what people come from all over the world to hear; and thirdly, because of its enormous popularity when broadcast (live) every Wednesday at 4 o'clock on Radio 3. Indeed, when the BBC has sought at different times to eliminate it from their schedules, the resulting uproar from a relatively small, but extremely vociferous, constituency has forced them to retreat.

The corresponding disadvantage of the popularity of Choral Evensong is, of course, that we seldom have the opportunity to listen to some of those magnificent settings of the morning canticles, Te Deum Laudamus and Benedicite Omnia Opera, Benedictus and Jubilate Deo. However, let us be profoundly thankful that the great Evensong tradition is being maintained so well in so many of our cathedrals: long may it flourish and, if I may misquote a verse of the National Anthem, may the politics and knavish tricks of misguided Deans and Chapters, or Provosts and Councils, be confounded and frustrated, should they be mindful at any time to pull out the plug marked 'Choral Evensong'.

Yet another threat to the tradition is one which I think can most conveniently be labelled 'political'. It was the received wisdom, even a few years ago, that the return to power of a Labour government would bring with it the virtual abolition of choir schools, not so unsubtly as by a deliberate act of closing down anything vaguely élitist, so much as by way of withdrawing their charitable status. The gradual move towards the centre which we have witnessed under the leadership successively of John Smith and Tony Blair has made this a far less likely scenario, but who would dare to forecast that some future political polarisation, which would bring about the same effect, is totally unthinkable?

* * *

Those, then, are some of the problems, and some of the things that might well be perceived as, at least potentially, threats to the Christian musical tradition in our cathedrals. It might interest you to know that, partly in response to some of the difficulties which beset us, and partly as a more positive way of pressing ahead, a number of bodies have been created over the years to support the work of cathedral musicians. Let me remind you, briefly, of five of them, and what they aim to achieve.

First, there is the COA, the Cathedral Organists' Association, which has been around since the 1930s, and has done an enormous amount to obtain improvements in the working conditions, salaries, pensions, housing and contracts of its members.

Secondly, the Friends of Cathedral Music, the FCM, which I am pleased to say was founded (in the mid 1950s) by a former Priest Vicar of the Cathedral in which I serve, and has made grants to cathedral and collegiate choirs of a sum approaching the half-million mark.

Thirdly, the Choir Schools' Association, the CSA, which brings together such diverse institutions as Westminster Abbey, the only place now to have a school solely for its own choristers, the Comprehensive School of Southwell Minster, and two Roman Catholic Schools, as well as all the more obvious choir schools of the York, Exeter and Salisbury brand. The existence of these schools, some of which go back to pre-Conquest days, is highly significant in the maintenance of the choral tradition. They cost a huge amount to run and yet the parental contribution averages under 50% and can be virtually nil. At Truro, for instance, the parents only pay one quarter of the fees. There is no doubt that, from the musical standpoint, there is a tremendous advantage in having all the choristers educated at the same school.

Fourthly, there is the Federation of Cathedral Old Choristers' Association, formed in 1910, to promote friendship among its members and to assist in maintaining and improving the high standard of cathedral music.

The fifth body is a relatively latecomer on the scene and

was until recently known as the Deans, Provosts and Organist Working Party. Following a restructuring, it is now called the Cathedral Music Working Party and has as its members 5 Deans or Provosts, 5 Cathedral Organists, 5 Cathedral Precentors, the Chairman of the Choir Schools' Association and the Director of the Royal School of Church Music, who acts as its Secretary. To give you some idea of the ground it covers, its agendas within recent years have included the appraisal of church musicians, the commissioning of new music, sponsorship and other sources of funding, girls in cathedral choirs, contracts for organists, the recruitment of choristers and lay clerks, the Purcell tercentenary, contemporary music and current liturgical trends, payments for broadcasts, the relationship between Cathedral and Diocese, the Archbishops' Commission on Church Music, the Archbishops' Commission on Cathedrals, and links with the RSCM.

The RSCM is itself, of course, very much concerned with, and involved in, the music of cathedrals and several of its Area Chairmen work in cathedrals.

* * *

The report *In Tune with Heaven* states that cathedrals...

> represent a continuity of worship and music stretching back to a period well before the Reformation. They have had an enormous influence on the music of this country, both sacred and secular, thanks to modern communications. The distinctive contribution which our cathedrals make to western culture is the more significant because of a world-wide recognition that they represent something unique.

The report adds that:

> in spite of the turmoil of the late twentieth century, cathedrals have shown both resilience and consistency. They have had to face the demands of liturgical change, increasing pressures from tourism, media attention, financial constraints and the expensive upkeep of large and expensive buildings. But they have survived with equanimity and, indeed, with enhanced prestige.

That more recent archiepiscopally-commissioned report, *Heritage and Renewal*, is also highly affirmative:

> During our visits to cathedrals we were delighted by the very high standards of liturgy and music. When we asked individuals what was specially good about their cathedral, the first answer was invariably the music [not the clergy, you'll notice]. Musical standards have probably never been higher.

This could very easily lead to complacency, to the attitude that says or implies that all is well, we have weathered many a storm, we have kept the heritage intact, and now we can rest awhile. The very act of putting it into such words is, I trust, more than enough to demonstrate that the price of this priceless piece of tradition is eternal vigilance, the determination not merely to maintain it, but to improve it in every legitimate way.

I hope you realise that much of this depends on the encouragement of people such as yourselves, who value the invaluable, who feel that they have a share in the musical tradition of our cathedrals, and who are happy to adopt for themselves those words of St Paul, *Psallam spiritu et mente*.

3

Cathedrals and Tourism

RICHARD LEWIS
The Dean of Wells

The Cathedral was full although I cannot remember the actual event for which so great a number had come for worship and thanksgiving. The Dean and Chapter had been taken to the West End, there to receive the Mayor and others and so the service could begin. There was that usual air of quiet expectancy that most often descends on such a gathering. A visitor came through the door and, no doubt because I was nearest, came up to me and asked, in all innocence, 'Is this place owned by the National Trust?' The prospect of that visitor running screaming down Wells High Street pursued by an enraged Dean is still pleasant to contemplate. Had I thought about it a little longer I should of course have been much more canny and indeed sensible, said, 'yes it was', and charged him £4.50 to come in. I smiled instead, but confess I cannot remember what banal words I used. I feel slightly better about that person since a colleague recounted only the other day that someone came in enquiring if 'this was the Town Hall' and 'where was the antiques fair?'

Our generation has had to live with a greater pace of change than any generation before, or so it seems. The demand for an unmoving church is understandable but it is an illusion. The church has always been a moving church and we can contemplate it without anxiety. The image of the pilgrim church is a striking one and very appropriate for a church wishing to take evangelism seriously in this age of mobility. It is appropriate too for faith communities who are carving themselves new life and new hopes in a fragmenting, restless and uncertain world. As part of this restlessness, enabled no doubt by increased leisure, as well as driven by a quest for meaning and purpose, more people than ever are visiting our cathedrals. In cathedral circles there is a verse which runs, 'I am a pilgrim, you are a visitor, he is a tourist'.

The image of movement and restlessness contrasts with the solidity, the permanence, the power and the dominance of the great European cathedrals of which the English cathedrals are, some would say, supreme and unique examples. It is important to state again and again that they existed in the past as they exist today for the primary purpose of the worship of God. This is what they are for. Yet in saying that I am aware they are much more than that in the formal sense; that the worship of God, as well as the perception of him within a cathedral, as elsewhere, is infinitely more subtle than words or liturgy can convey. In a cathedral God may be discerned within the very stones themselves; they are *inspired* with His Spirit. Within the Christian community that may seem self-evident but not to all. I can bear witness to many examples of dissatisfaction and complaint from visitors when, for example general movement in part or all of the cathedral is discouraged because worship is taking place. This has to do with sacred space and holy ground.

Close to that primary purpose there is a secondary reason for a cathedral's existence. It is the very reason which gives its name. It is this: to house and represent the teaching authority, 'the cathedral', the 'seat' of the Bishop. It is a matter of conjecture whether Bishops are seen more frequently in the cathedral than their predecessors of other centuries. They travel their diocese more and yet, unlike many predecessors of other centuries are more resident there as well. The visits made by the Archbishops' Commission on Cathedrals in 1992 discovered all cathedrals take seriously their teaching function and those with a large number of tourists are alive to the need and aware of the opportunities presented to them to make an apologetic for the Christian faith. 'In one sense,' says the newly published Report of the Archbishops' Commission, 'a cathedral must be allowed to speak for itself, on its own terms, and yet buildings, like people, need help if they are to speak in a language which communicates.'[1] It is doubtful if we can take for granted any longer that there is a common language in matters of faith. In this nation it is possible to make the case that we are already not one, but two, generations separated from holy things and the words and symbols that accompany them; separated too from the scriptures from whose inspiration craftsmen's art and music's measure alike illuminated both the fabric and the holy drama that took place within it. The stories are simply not known to so many any longer.

The reason for the monumental structure of the ancient cathedral is rather more uncertain. To the greater glory of God the perfection of proportion and soaring vaults spoke eloquently. 'But can God indeed dwell on earth?' prays Solomon. 'Heaven itself, the highest heaven, cannot contain you; how much less this house that I have built.'[2] Pride too played a part no doubt in the building of a cathedral, and rivalry as well. Those that were shrines in which rested the remains of saints and holy people not only increased the status of the Bishop but also were special places of pilgrimage for the faithful and, indeed, the not so faithful.

Possibly therefore the large cathedrals that in a number of places replaced the early, smaller, Saxon or Celtic ones, had to be built to a size that would accommodate those pilgrims and visitors as well as the associated activity and industries, both necessary and commercially needed to sustain them. The simple truth that they were built solely to the greater glory of God is probably at odds with the politics of the time. The evidence from archives would appear to suggest that the lives of the builders, and those who worked in them, were neither more nor less devout than their contemporaries, or perhaps even ours. The Chain Gate Bridge at Wells linking

Vicars Close where the Choir lived (and live still) was, so goes the tale, constructed to release the men from the temptation of going to the 'red light' district in St Thomas' Street a mere hundred metres away. For those employed as builders and the associated industries the construction of a cathedral was a means to earn a living. Devotion in short and brutish lives may have been no greater than now. The carving of 'green men' and other symbols of the 'old religion', found in many cathedrals, indicated both a double insurance and also a sense of humour about things divine. Money was then, as now, a problem and cathedrals needed the gifts of their visitors as well as the monuments to benefactors. The evidence also seems to indicate that from early times tourism, for that is what we would call it now, was a strong feature in their life. 'The medieval past is hedged with romantic inventions mostly of nineteenth century origin and it is through the screen of interpretation still provided by this largely fictional understanding that cathedrals of the time are assessed.'[3]

The cathedral is a sign and symbol of religious roots and is a testimony to the rich diversity of spiritual expression. Its calling within the church is unique, standing now on the border of the religious and secular worlds in a way many parish churches are no longer able to do. It is the largest 'sacred space' people ever enter, or, as my Head Virger has been heard to mutter of Wells, 'The largest umbrella in Somerset'. It affirms and encourages a wide expression of religious life and must support the religious and spiritual quest of different groups and individuals as well as maintaining its own domestic round of worship and prayer. The proposition that a cathedral (like its smaller sister, a parish church) is the house of God and is inviolate because of this, is a matter now more in dispute than in earlier times. I received a letter last year from a person who thinks it is disgraceful spending 'all that money on Wells Cathedral. Surely the proper thing to do is to sell the cathedral to a builder to turn into flats and use the money to feed the homeless and hungry'. It is not an attractive proposition and I suspect the economics are such that the hungry and homeless would have little left over for them.

Some Christian groups, those, for instance, who hire cinemas or conference centres for regular worship perhaps sit lightly on the concept of the permanence and glory of God's House but the instinct to locate Almighty God in place is primitive, basic and scriptural. Before ever we considered the role of the Temple in Jerusalem as the focus of religious and national hopes and aspirations, as well as its place in the consciousness of the Jews and of course of Jesus, I would need to take you much further back in time and religious consciousness.

So, to anchor your thinking firmly within the Scriptures I can do no better than direct your minds and imagination to those years represented by the book of Genesis. Leaving aside the wandering Abraham, in whose own God-led journeying place was a significant feature, I make the strong claim that the first person who came to a holy place and built there God's House and indeed named it as such, Bethel, 'God's House', was Jacob. Those who come to a cathedral come by many roads and many faiths and for many different reasons. Jacob came there not particularly as a tourist. He came almost by accident as one seeking protection and sanctuary to a 'certain shrine... He stopped for the night. He took one of the stones there and, using it as a pillow under his head, he lay down to sleep. In a dream he saw a ladder, which rested on the ground with its top reaching to heaven, and angels of God were going up and down on it'.[4]

That account has special meaning for me of course because I know exactly what he means. Going to the Chapter House in Wells 'a tongue of stone curves upwards into an astonishing octagon, its light shattered over the floor by traceried windows. In the middle, a huge pillar of tightly clasped shafts soars upwards to burst into 36 ribs. These seem to rise into the sky, joining the wall ribs like palm fronds waving in the breeze.' So wrote the journalist Simon Jenkins in *The Times*[5] in an article which did much justice to my Cathedral but little to the Dean and Chapter whom he castigated for not charging him to see it. To that subject I must return.

To return to Jacob. When he 'woke from his sleep he

said, "Truly the Lord is in this place, and I did not know it". He was awe-struck and said, "How awesome is this place! This is none other than the house of God: it is the gateway to heaven." Before leaving the next day he set up stones as a permanent mark of the presence of God.'[6] Was this the first cathedral?

We know too of the importance of the Temple in Jewish history, of its building, and of its destruction and rebuilding and its destruction again. We know of its significance as a place of pilgrimage for Mary, Joseph and the young boy Jesus and how Jerusalem was thronged with pilgrims as Jesus made his fateful journey into Holy Week.

History also indicates that whenever the Christian Church emerged from periods of persecution it began to build, rebuild or claim again for their own places in which the 'Holy' is located. Evidence from Eastern Europe and Russia supports that view. Pilgrimage too has an equally long and honourable tradition from as early as the fourth century to Jerusalem; then Rome and Constantinople; then to national shrines of which, in England, Canterbury was the foremost. In medieval times pilgrims were by far the most numerous of travellers. In as yet unpublished data the historian and writer Henry Hobhouse observes that more than 10% of the adult male population made some kind of journey as a pilgrim... 'At one time, it was held necessary for every priest, monk or nun to have made a pilgrimage, and in some places, these could represent up to 30% of the adult population.'

Thus I come to remind you that the primary role of a cathedral is not, in the first instance a tourist attraction. It is a place of worship; it is a community of living faith. This primary purpose is recognised in England and it is enshrined in law as clause 1 of the 1990 Cathedrals Measure. Anybody having care and conservation shall have 'due regard to the fact that the cathedral church is the seat of the bishop and a centre of worship and mission.'[7] That above all else is what a cathedral is for and the offering of worship is the daily concern of the Dean and Chapter.

In this I am of all persons the most fortunate. Before

7.30am on nearly every day of the year I enter my Cathedral by way of the North Porch. On the outside of the porch I am greeted in time-worn stone of exquisite medieval carving by the story of the East Anglian defender of the faith who perished at the hands of the invader, Edmund, King and Martyr. For pilgrim and community alike the tale of blood poured out, and sacrifice made, has been told silently for 800 years. That story is told in each cathedral in stone and wood and brass and inscribed words of past faithfulness and present life and worship. As I go into the Cathedral at that often silent and lonely hour and walk the aisle to the Lady Chapel for morning prayer, it is to step into faith. It is to be touched by both time and the eternal, to be surrounded by the prayer of those who have passed that way before; whose prayer seemingly enriches and soaks the stone and canopied arches.

That may be considered too romantic a view; yet in the Archbishops' Commission on Cathedrals they are described as shop windows of the Church of England. What is true, in a nation that has in so many ways become disconnected not only with its church but with its faith as well, is that many people get their ideas about the church from what goes on in its cathedrals. They are frequently seen on television screens; they are the setting for large public occasions of thanksgiving or grief. They are moreover visited by large numbers of people. In 1992 The English Tourist Board estimated that of 68.7 million visits made to historic buildings nearly half of those were to cathedrals and churches. Of that latter figure, 14.5 million visited Anglican cathedrals.[8] We shall be naive in thinking that all, or even most are pilgrims in an identifiable Christian sense. In a survey done for the Archbishops' Commission, 41% claimed membership of the Church of England but 27% said they were not members of a church.[9] With such numbers I conclude that cathedrals are a vital ingredient in any strategy for mission, witness and evangelism by the church.

The present social and economic, spiritual and theological context in which cathedrals 'live and move and have their being' is crucial to any understanding of their relationship with any who come within their shadow. The present context is one dominated by the media. It is now a deeply pagan media where fantasies, especially dark fantasies, are explored. Now the cathedral neither engages in mission nor does its evangelisation in a void unconnected with what is happening around them however much that is the impression some may wish to understand. Ours is an age of the sound byte, the fast fading visual image. It is an age where very complex thoughts and ideas are reduced to single sentences and in such an age cathedrals are peculiarly placed. On the one hand their vast spaces, rich carvings, strong pillars, graceful arches, odour of sanctity, are the medieval equivalent of today's televisual age. On the other hand the electronic media, heard and seen by nearly everyone, is where people now learn the stories of the community, where they explore its myths and where its fears are made manifest in anything but the holy.

Such a role was once played by the cathedrals and any strategy now developed cannot be like a commercial promotion, otherwise we should organise ourselves as a cross between the Museum of London and Disneyland. (It is a charge sometimes levelled.) The temptation is born of the demands of the place and it is ever present. It permeates the whole. In evidence to the Commission the English Tourist Board said the 'the emphasis of the interpretation is on the fabric of the building including the stained glass, the tombs and the brasses. Relatively less attention appears to be given to the interpretation of the spiritual, cultural and social roles of the cathedrals.'[10] If this is so, it will be understood as a damning indictment. If it is true, it must provide the agenda for sharp remedial action.

The Christian community believes is has something to offer to the world. The same tensions, the same disagreements, the same despair and quarrelsomeness, is present in the Christian community because it is made up of fallible human persons. But the cathedral community must, if it is to be faithful, have an inner life and inner vision. Has it learnt anything about the art of the possible? Has it learned anything about forgiveness? Has it any good news to give? Is it able to move from self-interest and power-seeking, prejudice and jealousy, in its dealing with one another to openness, understanding, forgiveness and respect, partnership, friend-ship, love? This the tourist who is sometimes more open even than the pilgrim is able to sense because it is at the heart of the community. Forgiveness, love, humour. Our forefathers who built the medieval cathedrals knew there was a 'need for understanding of their cosmological and theological premises, and knowledge of the fact that geometry expressed in matter was perceived as a mirror of celestial harmony.'[11] Such harmony, such perfection, is not now understood nor is it taken for granted. The visitor will absorb any such har-mony mostly from the people who love and work within the cathedral. Sensitive interpretation and understanding is essential for all involved in visitors and their management.

Focus then needs to be on the story and not so much on the 'when' of the buildings. Any strategy to be authentic to the Cathedral's purpose must take seriously present responsi-bilities. Always this needs to be a response to what God has done and continues to do in his creation. If our fundamental belief is that the whole of created order is called to worship, cathedrals have a special privilege and duty to help people to say their 'yes'. We use that which is given and in the case of most cathedrals the very first gift to the traveller is the space itself, sacred space. For many this is the biggest building they have entered that day – perhaps ever. Yet cathedrals are reluc-tant to be seen to be bound up in the tourist industry. They know the potential for destruction that exists: destruction of peace and holiness in even such a great space simply heaving with people looking; destruction too of the very fine fabric that has stood these centuries. I simply have to say we must see this in terms of opportunity and not of problem, and any theology of the Incarnation cannot but include the complex-ities of the age so represented by people on the move as never before. Being on the move they affect the places they come to and, please God, are affected by them in return.

So a cathedral evokes a reaction, a response. When tak-

ing visitors around the Cathedral in Liverpool the architect
Giles Scott used to say, 'Do not look at my arches, look at my
spaces'. On his visit to that same cathedral Sir John Betjeman
exclaimed 'This is one of the great building of the world. The
impression of vastness, of strength and height no words can
describe. Suddenly one sees that the greatest art of architecture that lifts one up and turns one into a king, yet compels
reverence, is the art of enclosing space.'[12] It is not always easy
to find space in today's crowded world but space is important. Grace and space go together. 'O Lord, set my feet in a
large room' is a prayer for our time and a worthy prayer for
the pilgrim to a cathedral. Observe closely people coming
into a cathedral. Many simply stand. This is particularly true
when worship is already taking place. Sacred space is significant at unconscious levels. It is sacred space for 'the ground
on which you stand is holy ground'.[13] Finding silence and
peace is of course another matter. The very words 'crowds'
and 'crowded' invite another response for the tourist as dis-
tinct from the pilgrim who knows that cathedrals are part of
the nation's heritage. That is what they are there for and the
tramp of their feet renders a cathedral anything but a still
centre. There is too a growing tension between the care of
ancient fabric and replacement with new for old as in the case
of the steps in the Chapter House at Wells.

The cathedral – it is theirs, then; they are welcome, they
can walk in it unhindered. But what is it for? I have no rosy
view of why people come. 'Not another Cathedral', said one
tired coach member, 'it's the third today'. 'This is Salisbury',
said the coach driver as he deposited his charges in Wells
Market Square. 'I'll pick you up in an hour and we'll go on
to Winchester.' It is easy to hold a sentimental view of the reason for a person's visit and yet the very presence of tourists
sets an agenda for the cathedral's work.

The very stones themselves can articulate what words
cannot say. It is one of the ironies of the Christian faith that,
whereas God is not to be confined to any particular place,
nonetheless because the stream is deeper than Christian consciousness His presence is enshrined in places of great beauty

and often antiquity that are dedicated to His honour. It is also another irony that, although rooted in Christian teaching is the belief in God who seeks relationships with his creation, yet many millions alive today, and countless before that, make pilgrimage to find Him in separated and holy places. In cathedrals then, for all these centuries prayer has been offered. Here praises to God have been sung, day in and day out. By simply **being** it declares itself to be different, to be set apart, to be holy.

Cathedrals are witnesses, silent sermons in stone, and for this they are well suited. Their very scale tells of a people who know they cannot accomplish perfection or indeed anything in their own strength. Cathedrals stand mute sentinels of the belief of men and women in the eternal. They are a testimony to what God has done and what he is. They are to be spoken in the same breath as a Mozart Mass, a Beethoven Symphony or the Brahms Requiem. A Rembrandt, a Constable, a Turner. The writer of St Luke recalls Jesus telling his Disciples that 'you are witnesses to these things.'[14] Cathedrals are true witnesses to resurrection not necessarily by the personal lives of their builders, nor of those who have lived and worked in them throughout history, though many have been women and men of great holiness. No, they are rendered holy by being what they claim to be and by what they are.

If the very stones cry glory so too their history tells the church's story through the lives of individual Christians. Self-evident you may think if you live and work surrounded by the saints and sinners of the past in a Cathedral close. It may not be so obvious to the visitor who may come as on a visit to a museum. Travelling to and from London from the west I pass by Stonehenge and see great numbers gazing on those silent stones and hidden history. Practically nothing is really known about those for whom the stones were significant. I should not too readily suppose that many who visit our great cathedral look with any greater understanding. This factor sets a different programme for cathedrals of the present day than was the case until the middle part of this century. Until then there were more common assumptions, more shared inheritance, more general acceptance of Christian roots.

The stark reality of the present day is not of a nation less religious but rather more gullible. A people, in the words of the prophet Jeremiah, 'that have forsaken me, swearing by gods that are no gods... They have denied the Lord saying, "he does not matter, no harm will come to us, we shall see neither sword nor famine. The prophets will prove mere wind, the word is not in them".'[15]

That is on one side. On the other is perhaps a church that behaves as if revolutions in knowledge, in media, in communication, in human and behavioural sciences, have not taken place. The Commission's report utters a warning when it offers the opinion that 'if organisations feel they have to come only on the cathedral's terms, it should not cause surprise if the next generation does not ask to come at all'.[16]

If we are a nation therefore and a culture that has been and is moving so rapidly away from its Christian inheritance, we may also question the claim to the reality of a Christian nation. The Commission's report goes on to say clearly that 'the living purpose of the cathedral needs to be made explicit – not just saying that the people of the past built the cathedral because of their faith but saying what the faith was and is'.[17]

'For many in the western world today it may lead to a kind of wistful fellow-travelling with religion, able neither to accept it nor wholly to dismiss it, retaining a memory of old tales of deity kept echoing in the caverns of the mind more by poetry than by argument.'[18] I would like also to go on to say that God is kept alive more by people's lives and the lives of the community of faith. I know too that the best visitor care will not be judged by the amount done or said but by the extent to which visitors leave with a sense of relationship to what they have seen and the people who live in it.[19] In this comparisons with Benedictine hospitality are appropriate. Those who travel to cathedrals are not ready perhaps to admit readily to the God-shaped hole in their lives but it may be the work of the cathedral community to demonstrate that, for them, the whole can be filled.

A coherent view of life must of course take account of death even in an age that has been described as an age of unfaith. Here again an ancient cathedral, more than churchyard or cemetery, more than parish church, demonstrates history and mortality deeply entwined in the material and on a scale that evokes wonder from those who come.

But it is not just stone, however beautifully configured. The gospel is incarnate, the word made flesh, is within the people and the community who live and worship and, as well, he is within those who come. Considerable resources of people, time and energy as well as money are committed to the ministry of welcome and hospitality in any cathedral with a large number of visitors. The total spend over all cathedrals, according to Archbishops' Commission data, is probably in excess of 25% of expenditure or some £10 million per annum.

Cathedrals do not always get it right, of that I am acutely conscious. They do not communicate as well as they might. They are always willing to listen and to learn. So when, after taking an excellent guided tour, a North American visitor comes to the Information Desk and asks, 'What denomination is this Church?', I realise a small but significant bit of information needs to be added to the Guide's notes for I am conscious that our particular calling is indeed to represent in our special way the historic church of the nation and I am extremely proud of that fact.

I cite this minute incident as a means of illustrating the twin dilemma a cathedral faces in relation to its visitors. In the case of Wells this is in excess of 350,000. Tourists, Pilgrims, Visitors, what **are** we to call them?, are of great significance to our cathedrals. One thing we may not do and that is to make any assumptions that those who come inside the cathedral know anything about or share even remotely the faith for which the cathedral stands. Those who come are of significance for their own sakes and also for the opportunities of demonstrating Christian life in worship, welcome and hospitality; for the opportunities for telling the Christian story through the images, the furniture, the shape and size of the sacred space and the very stones of the cathedral itself; for the opportunities of direct teaching about the faith in the questions that are answered and asked in return.

Our Tourists, Visitors, Pilgrims are of significance too because they represent and they **have** to represent a major source of income. And here many a Dean is also heard to mutter, 'not nearly major enough'. I had better lay my cards on the table. I do not now consider the moral and theological high ground belongs to those who champion free entry to our cathedrals. Where it is practical or necessary it is perfectly proper to consider a formal charge to enter a cathedral. There are different theologies to be brought to bear and there is a tension between them. Clearly there will be the interests of some, especially those who come for prayer, worship or consolation, that need to be sensitively considered, but what a charge does do is free those whose care the cathedral is to concentrate on the experience that tourist has, not the least of which is the telling of the Christian story.

Charges are now becoming commonplace and our society has come to expect to pay at the point of delivery for so many things. I believe to equate what a visitor donates with God's free grace is inadequate theology. That is especially true when the average gift is between 40 and 50p and that is generally on the top side. I am far more convinced by a theology that speaks of costly grace and a faith that demands not just some of me but all. At present Deans and Chapters of those cathedrals with considerable tourist numbers spend considerable time and energy devising just those right words for the signs that will persuade a visitor to give rather than for the interpretation of the building. I therefore confess to you the shame I felt when the person on the Information desk said the other day that such and such a group of people had arrived as an unbooked tour and my response was quite simply, 'Did you persuade them to pay?' This is not worthy and it is not right. Far better I judge to be open and honest. In the end there is no free visit. The only question is who pays. If cathedrals are willing to take taxpayers' money through Heritage Grants they are already taking enforced payment and Government is entitled to ask what cathedrals are doing to help themselves.

In *The Times* article quoted previously Simon Jenkins wrote of Wells that he could see it for nothing. 'If the Dean and Chapter can afford me this luxury, good for them. I will praise and magnify their name. But I know they cannot.' I am under no illusion. Charge will change the relationship between the cathedral and its visitors but it can be seen as opportunity and not as regression.

The issue raises considerable heat though often not much light. The hard truth is that if visitors to cathedrals gave £1 per head the financial position would be transformed. If they were to give the £1.50 invited cathedrals could turn to even more effective witness. In truth it is a pathetically small amount and comes to little more than a begging bowl at the door of heaven to catch the remnants that fall from the rich persons' table. Not to give even at that level is stark evidence of a pervading sin of ungenerosity which so easily affects us all.

Continuing at the warm heart of the cathedral is its daily praise of God. The English Cathedrals, wonderful masterpieces of design and art, tellers of the story of the faith, singers of the praises of God, friendly roof to any who come for shelter are not ancient monuments. They are living communities whose sole purpose is to inspire the hearts and spirits of many millions of persons year by year and lift them so high that they may see, albeit through the glass darkly, the face of Christ and receive a transforming vision of the divine.

Some may consider that Pilgrim and Tourist are interchangeable terms. A pilgrim is self-defined as one who is making a spiritual journey and although some tourists may seek a spiritual dimension implicit in a visit to a cathedral, yet they own to no commitment by word or deed to Christian things. Indeed there is sometimes acute embarrassment at the public reading of prayers although a pilgrimage of the devout with their priest and candle moving to different parts of the cathedral will always evoke considerable interest and no little respect. 'Praise God in his holy place, praise him in the mighty vault of heaven', prays the Psalmist,[20] and I recall the impact on a quite crowded cloister at the sight and sound of some twenty people, visitors from somewhere on the Pacific ring walking in the cloister singing a hymn. It was unselfconscious and it was inspiring.

To sum up. Cathedrals are good news. They are Gospel. They have a problem. The Gospel is about people and kingdom matters. Cathedrals present themselves as huge and towering awesome buildings. Cathedrals drip with the past and much energy goes into presenting the past within them and keeping the past alive. The Gospel is about newness of life in the present and the looking forward. The Cathedral can be seen as a parable of faith, testimony to the heights of the human spirit in art and design and scale, signs of an engodded creation, of permanent things in an impermanent world, of the losing of self in wonder, love and praise in order to find the Word at the heart of creation. The Cathedral must speak for itself and we whose work is bound up with its life must be enablers so that our visitors may feel at home with us in order that they may feel at home with God in Christ. 'He it is whom we proclaim. We teach everyone and instruct everyone in all the ways of wisdom, so as to present each one of you as a mature member of Christ's body. To this end I am toiling strenuously with the the energy and power of Christ at work in me.'[21]

Notes

1. Page 35, para 61 Heritage and Renewal, The Report of the Archbishops' Commission on Cathedrals Church House Publishing 1994
2. Kings 8, 37
3. Heritage and Renewal: Note on the Historical Background, page 190, para 5
4. Genesis 28 verse 10 et seq.
5. The Times, 20 August 1994
6. Genesis 28
7. Care of Cathedrals Measure 1990
8. English Tourist Board Survey quoted in Heritage and Renewal, page 136
9. Church Statistical Unit Survey, quote in Heritage and Renewal, page 141
10. English Tourist Board. Evidence to the Archbishops' Commission, para 314
11. Dr Friedhelm Hoffmann, 1991: Address to the Annual Conference for the Pilgrim's Association
12. Quoted by Dean Riley of Manchester in Commission papers
13. Genesis ch 3 vs 5

14. Luke 24 48
15. Jeremiah 5, 7 & 12
16. Heritage and Renewal, page 19 para 8
17. Heritage and Renewal, page 33 para 53
18. John Polkinhorne, Science and Christian Belief, SPCK 1994
19. Canon Peter Brett: Evidence to the Commission
20. Psalm 150 vs 1
21. Colossians ch 1 vs 28 et seq.

4

Cathedrals and Christian Imagination

HUGH DICKINSON
The Dean of Salisbury

Our daughter's room is in one of the attics in the Deanery. It has a small casement window looking out through the branches of a lime tree to the Gothic windows and pinnacles of the great grey building across the wide lawns of the Close. In spite of its massive size the Cathedral is a curiously light structure. Its dominant features are repeated verticals. At all three levels of the nave, triforium and clerestory its pointed windows look like apertures left for space rockets, as if the whole thing might be preparing for take off. The verticals continue up the narrow buttresses and then on up into the central tower, and then – you have to crane your neck back – even higher into the slender soaring spire. 'Reach for the sky', it seems to say, 'that is where we come from.' It is easy to think that it might after all be an abandoned space ship which landed here in the thirteenth Century. Turn it on its side and give it a backcloth of slowly wheeling stars and it would make a fine special effects space craft for *Star Wars* or a *Space Odyssey*.

But now it is well and truly grounded. The upper tower and spire alone – probably an afterthought to the original design – added an extra 6,000 tons of masonry to the huge building. Someone has done a calculation of the total weight of stone pressing down on to the bed of gravel which is its only natural foundation. I won't bother you with the total. Figures are death to the imagination. They can only tell you of its dead weight.

This building is very much alive. Its face can wear as many moods as the English weather or a sensitive woman. It can float in early summer mists or lower angrily under November skies. It is sometimes pale ochre or pink, sometimes grey or brown, sometimes silver; and there is one magical moment, after the sun has set in a clear sky, when the floodlights have come on, but before the daylight is quite gone, when it turns green and seems to hover just above the level surface of the lawns. It is alive and numinous.

There are rumours of restless spirits in some of the old houses round the Close, and I once asked our daughter whether she was sleeping peacefully in her little attic room, for her brother has always refused to sleep up there. She paused for a moment to reflect. 'Yes,' she said, 'I think so. But I'm always aware of the shadow of the spire across my dreams.'

The shadow of the spire across our dreams. These buildings have a mysterious power to colour the way we think about ourselves, our history and our world. They have an architectonic force in the corporate imagination which stretches far beyond the immediate penumbra of their shadows. In his strange novel *Enigmas of Arrival* V.S. Naipaul tells of his own experience of growing up as an Asian child on an island in the West Indies. He sat in a makeshift classroom in a rough village school where the only thing to fire his imagination was a reproduction of a Constable landscape painting of Salisbury Cathedral. In that unlikely tropical setting the image of the spire rising among the surrounding elm trees so imprinted itself on his mind that it seemed almost like a homecoming when he arrived to settle within sight of it.

In that novel Naipaul hardly speaks of the Cathedral; he describes in obsessively observed detail the hedges and lanes and woods of the Woodford Valley a mile or two north of the City through which he took his daily compulsive walks up the drove road to Stonehenge. But even up that ancient landscape the spire still casts a long shadow, a sharp thorn pricking the skyline to the south. The Avon winding through the water meadows is drawn southwards to pass under the walls of the Close. Even the sacred circle of Stonehenge up on the open Plain seems to have surrendered some of its old magical powers to this new edifice in the valley where five rivers meet. It's as if all the primaeval energies of the neolithic barrows and dolmens of the Wessex downland and their psychic force had drained away down the chalkland streams to be gathered in by the gravitational pull of this huge mass of stone. You don't have to be fey or a poetic visionary like Wordsworth to sense that Stonehenge is a kind of lens for psychic forces:

> Lines, circles, mounts, a mystery of shapes
> By which the Druids covertly expressed
> Their knowledge of the Heavens and imaged forth
> The constellations.

And, about Stonehenge:

> The pomp is for both worlds the living and the dead.

There's no doubt in my own mind that these great buildings do also have a powerful psychic penumbra. I don't think it is fanciful to speak of a cathedral's *daimon*; at least that is a useful image of the kind of force that seems to emanate from it, and of the effects it has on the human community around it. A *daimon*, you will recall, is a spiritual energy not quite impersonal, not quite good or bad, a kind of field of psychic force which certain places and certain people or institutions seem to gather to themselves. The Romans would say of a particular wood or cliff or pool '*Numen inest* – there is a Presence here'. Hence our English word 'numinous'. Houses too have spirits of their own, some kindly, some sad or malign; by which I do not mean for a moment to suggest they are haunted, though some are. That's an entirely different kind of thing. A home acquires a peaceful, kindly atmosphere from being lived in by gracious, gentle people, and that generous spirit persists maybe for centuries to nurture the spirits of later families.

The *daimon* of a cathedral is an altogether more powerful and scary thing. It seems to be able to plug into the psyches of individuals and groups of people, particularly those living close to it or working constantly in its shadow, and it can do strange things to otherwise good and ordinary men and women. It's as if it enlarges or exaggerates the existing spiritual tempo of those who come within its field of force. Because of our fallen nature I think we are much more vulnerable to its distortions and less skilled at using its creative energies than we would like to think. It is no secret that the personal relationships of some Deans and Canons in and around our English cathedrals have been bitter and destructive. People who in any other setting would be found to be kindly and generous seem to be taken over by a spirit of contention which erodes their virtues and exaggerates their faults. The *daimon* has got its tentacles into them and is manipulating them.

Of course it does not have to be so; there are enough instances of exemplary Christian fellowship in cathedral Chapters to make that plain. And I am happy and immensely privileged to live and work in a place in which our relationships are generally marked by candour and transparency, and by a mutual regard and care which means we can speak of being a Christian community without too much irony.

But from where does this *daimon* get its power? Great physical structures, whether natural or man-made, attract intense projections from the human community, especially those close to them. In an abstract way we all know the symbolic significance of vertical erections. But only those who have made the hazardous exploration of the unconscious of human groups or individuals or their own will have a gut feeling for the power great buildings exercise in our psyche.

The cathedral is potency and beauty and sacred space all rolled into one. The local community and visitors from distant places have all sorts of fantasies about it and about those who serve it. People dream about it just as they do about the Queen. It's almost as if they hand over part of their own inner world to it in a gesture of submission or dependence.

Philip Larkin gets it brilliantly right; he writes of one empty church:

> A serious house on serious earth it is,
> In whose blent air all our compulsions meet,
> Are recognised, and robed as destinies.
> And that much never can be obsolete...

Again – it is hard to be sure what is fanciful and what is genuine sensibility – the building itself has been the locus of a constant stream of worship and music and intense prayer for more than seven centuries. If our houses acquire spirits from their inhabitants, maybe our holy places absorb into their very stones the vibrations of the human spirits who have longed and prayed and grieved so passionately within them. All that music – the concert is over, the choir has left its robes in the vestry and gone home to tea, the organ loft is locked up and the bellows flat and airless. Not a murmur of an echo of all that glorious sound is left hanging in the air. But century after century the pillars and arcades, the plain ashlar of the walls of the building, surely absorb something of the beauty and the passion that so often have for a short while filled the air in there.

If that is true of those who worship and sing there what of those who spent their lives – maybe lost their lives – on this extraordinary enterprise in the twelfth or thirteenth centuries? You can get a pretty good idea of what it must have been like from Edward Rutherford's huge novel entitled *Sarum*. The dust, sweat and and sheer physical force were the visible signs of a human community driven by a compelling dream. Hundreds upon hundreds of men gave their souls to the task of building a miracle for God. We have contemporary accounts of noblemen and villains together stripped to the waist pulling great stones either in silence or singing penitential psalms while the sweat, blood and grime ran down their chests. But at what cost?

William Golding in his novel *The Spire* has given us a somewhat highly-coloured picture of the intense obsession one master builder – Dean Jocelyn – might have had with this prodigious scheme. He and others round him become consumed by the Cathedral and its spire. It seems to take on a life of its own and to become a voracious monster, turning on its creator and sucking the blood out of him until he is a sick husk of a man redeemed at the end only by being broken. Even if that is not counted as evidence for the reality of the *daimon* it is imaginatively plausible.

In any case the writing and the reading of *The Spire* by so many millions of people also feeds the *daimon* of the place. It is greedy for attention, devotion and love. Indeed it is possible that by writing these words and reading them aloud to you I may be feeding it myself. Be that as it may, I and other colleagues in other cathedrals have admitted to one another that there have been times when we have felt that we were being eaten alive.

Size and beauty alone are not the whole story. The architects of Salisbury Cathedral were men of great intellectual power. It wasn't their purpose simply to put up a huge structure to satisfy the King's desire for grandiose religious buildings. The building was intended to have a carefully articulated symbolic significance here in the English landscape. So its measurements and proportions are calculated with great numerical exactness.

Since the Enlightenment in the eighteenth century we have quite lost any notion of the power of the symbolism of numbers. But to our ancestors of almost every other generation numbers had extraordinary potency. In part it was a proper sense of awe at the inherent beauty of mathematics and geometry; a kind of wonder and delight to discover that the length of a vibrating string and its harmonics or pitch are exactly related; that music and architecture are capable of mathematical correlations; that the spiral in the human knuckle bone and in the seed head of a sunflower and in a conch shell are exact logarithmic curves. But in part this delight in numbers was a way of importing some intelligible structure into a formless and incoherent world. Numbers ruled in Heaven as they do on Earth. The crystal spheres and their associated planets chimed together in exact numerical concordance, and consequently certain numbers carried particular potency – 3, 5, 7, 13. Even today there are some people who stay in bed if it is Friday the 13th!

You can see this obsessive interest in numbers and proportion in all sorts of places – in Egypt, in Assyria, in classical Greece and more familiarly in the pages of Scripture. The Evangelists were far more interested in numbers than most biblical scholars have been prepared to allow. Why else has St Mark listed thirteen disciples, thirteen healings and thirteen loaves of bread? I will not weary you with explanations, but just draw your attention to the quantity of symbolic numbers in the Book of the Revelation of St John the Divine or the Book of Daniel or the Prophet Ezekiel or the Book of Kings where the dimensions of Solomon's Temple are listed in minute detail.

All these ancient holy structures, The Great Pyramid, Stonehenge and Solomon's Temple, have attracted the attention of a multitude of both serious students and madmen trying to elucidate the symbolism or numerology of their architecture. Sir Isaac Newton spent as much time on his struggle to understand the numbers in the Book of Daniel as he did on the refraction of light, and thought the study of far greater importance. Happily we don't have to follow their tortuous footsteps, but need only note that the ancient world and the medieval world alike both believed that it was possible to create buildings whose architecture was not only representational of aspects of the cosmos but also acted as a kind of lens to bring heavenly resonances down to earth.

One fascinating instance of this is in the Parody Mass of the late fifteenth century composer Obrecht written to celebrate a festival in Cambrai Cathedral. The structure of the Mass is complex, but on close analysis has been shown to have formal features symbolising the Festival for which it was written, the dimensions of Cambrai Cathedral and the movements of the planets. To take part in such a ceremony was to participate in a truly Galactic Mass.

Perhaps we should now be commissioning for the Millennium new music to reflect the beautiful progression of the Periodic Table, the elegant equations which rule the interactions of quarks and gluons, and the mysteriously exact balance of subatomic forces which created mankind and the cosmos.

When we come to examine the dimensions and proportions of Salisbury Cathedral we should not be surprised to discover that its architects and builders were concerned to do something more than erect a beautiful and well-proportioned Church. The building is also an essay in Christian imagination with carefully calculated symbolisms. Tracing these symbolisms is not as difficult as elucidating the riddle of the Sphinx or the riddles of the Great Pyramid, and a number of essays have been attempted, but still our conclusions can never be certain.

Of one thing we can be reasonably sure. The present 'new' cathedral was built as a replacement for the two earlier great churches constructed a mile to the north on the heights of the Iron Age fortification now known as Old Sarum. The first of these earlier cathedrals was completed by Bishop Osmund in 1092 and was badly damaged in an immense storm five days after its final consecration. Osmund was the founding father of Salisbury as a great Christian centre, a man of extraordinary vision and ability whose sanctity and learning became a local legend. Admittedly it took three hundred years and a lot of bribery before his sanctity was formally recognised by canonisation, but long before that his potency as holy man and healer was widely revered and pilgrims began to gather to his shrine. The local memory of a saint and the physical presence of his bones in a gilded shrine creates a numinous holy place in which the powers of heaven are channelled into life on earth. T. S. Eliot puts it like this:

> The blood of thy martyrs and saints
> Shall enrich the earth, shall create the holy places.
> For wherever a saint has dwelt,
>   wherever a martyr has give his blood for the
>   blood of Christ,
> There is holy ground, and the sanctity shall not
>   depart from it,

Though armies trample over it, though sightseers
  come with guide books looking over it;
From such ground springs that which forever renews
  the earth,
Though it is for ever denied.

(Murder in the Cathedral)

It wasn't long before the rebuilding of Osmund's Church was begun. It was already a holy place and so Bishop Roger constructed a much grander edifice for a much enlarged community still gathered around the Saint's Shrine at Old Sarum. He was careful to incorporate parts of the earlier building in his own. Even so it didn't survive long. By 1217 tensions between the Bishop's people and the King's men in the surrounding fortress had become intolerable and the Pope was petitioned to sanction a move.

So when Bishop Poore finally got permission from Rome to build a new cathedral in the valley below Old Sarum on Marymead where five rivers meet, his first concern was to demonstrate that he wasn't leaving St Osmund behind. As soon as the Lady Chapel (known as the Trinity Chapel) was complete the bones and relics of the Saint were solemnly reinterred in a new glorious shrine east of the High Altar. This was now the place of potency, here was the gateway to the realm of Light.

Shifting the Saint's bones was not enough. The new Cathedral was to be a building in the new Gothic style, utterly different in feeling and aspect from the heavy Romanesque of the two earlier Norman buildings at Old Sarum. How could the architects signal that this was nevertheless still the same Holy Place reborn? That it partook in some way of the archetypal Holy Places of the Holy Land? Even more, that it was now a lens to focus the whole cosmos?

The most detailed analysis of the principles underlying the design of Salisbury Cathedral has been published in the report of the Royal Commission on Historical Monuments by Peter Kidson. We cannot at this point follow the fascinating intricacies of the measurements and their geometric relationships, but in summary it becomes clear that a number of overlapping and sometimes mutually contradictory symbolic systems were in the mind of the architects. They settled on a primarily quadrangular scheme but with many overlays of triangular proportions. Both square and triangle have metaphysical properties. The square represents God – Himself multiplied by Himself; the triangle the Holy Trinity. They opted for irrational numbers generated from polygons. To ensure there were golden sections at spiritually significant points they shunted the regular square pattern of bays in the Nave and Transepts as they moved into the Quire. They were careful to carry down from Old Sarum not just the stones but the basic module of thirty nine feet, chosen by Osmond himself.

They also used the dimensions of Bishop Roger's Romanesque apse to generate the plan of the Eastern arm of the Cathedral, so that there is a ghostly apsidal presence under the rigid quadrilaterals. The central generating point is right under the middle of the Eastern gable below which the Shrine of St Osmund was almost certainly originally located. The spiritual and psychic symbolism is inescapable. Not only St Osmund's bones, but the spiritual essence of his Cathedral and its sacramental life which spring from his presence are now embodied in the very stones of this great new building. Later the Saint was moved into the centre of the four delicate Purbeck marble shafts which hold up the vault of the Trinity Chapel, so the Shrine would look as if contained in a giant reliquary. It was glorious with a pomp of gold and jewelry, in sharp contrast to the austerity and absence of ornament in the building around it, which may have been a deliberate rebuke to Canterbury and the overkill (if you will excuse the modernism) around the tomb of St Thomas Becket. We need to remember that the whole building was also a theological statement in an intense debate going on across the whole of Europe between Nominalism and Realism, the sumptuousness of Abbot Suger and the austerity of St Bernard.

The elevation of the building and its proportions spring naturally out of the ground plan. Its width and the height of the apex of the vault are identical – it is built within a containing square. Every minute detail of the smallest components was a function of the dimension of the basic square. Treatises were current like that of Mattheus Roriczer in the fifteenth century detailing the progressive elaboration of logarithmic and geometric proportions. Clearly the builders of Salisbury Cathedral were already masonic adepts.

The West Front in particular shows this careful mathematical elaboration. This aspect of the Cathedral is at once its most complex and (at least in Pevsner's view) least aesthetically successful feature. It is altogether too fussy and its internal proportions don't really work. We forget sometimes that it was originally highly coloured – positively garish to our modern taste. In effect it must have looked like the front of an immense reliquary, which is exactly what it now was. All along its niches and arcades over-life-size figures of the saints gazed down at the crowds of earthlings gathering beneath them to celebrate some Holy Day. Apertures in the stone enabled the choir in the galleries within to sing out through the facade so the whole array of heavenly personages would seem to be in chorus too. As the Liturgical Procession began to wend its way into the dark aperture of the great West Doorway every Christian soul must have felt, 'This is indeed none other than the House of God, this is the Gate of Heaven'.

You may think that the geometric connections to the earlier cathedrals at Old Sarum are quite enough to be going on with. There is however some evidence that the builders may have had a more ancient archetypal building in mind as well. The Temple of Solomon in Jerusalem was the subject of much speculation among medieval scholars and builders. Abelard points out that the dimensions of the Temple corresponded to the harmonic proportions advocated by the Neoplatonists. It was Plato in the *Timaeus* who declared that this harmony, shared equally by music and architecture, lay at the very roots of the universe in the mind of God himself. God as Creator is often represented with a pair of compasses. To this day the Masonic Rites contain numerous references to the Temple. Its proportions were studied intensively and it is possible that echoes of them were carefully incorporated into the relationships between Nave and Choir or Choir and Presbytery. The Litany for the dedication of a new church included Old Testament readings about the building of Solomon's Temple; in manuscripts the heavenly Jerusalem was portrayed as a Gothic cathedral.

So as their liturgical procession wound into the shadowy and subaqueous light of the interior of the building our medieval ancestors would have felt themselves moving into a vibrant sacred space, the arena of the dialogue between Heaven and Earth. The hierarchies of human and divine order so eloquently described by Pseudo Dionysius were made visible and audible. For the interior of the building now becomes a microcosm of the universe, an enclosed space of concentric crystal spheres, each attended by a troupe of angels. These spheres beam down their sweet influences upon the world of mortals below humming as they turn and – ideally – evoking an echoing murmur in the human spirit.

> Sit, Jessica – look how the floor of Heaven
> Is thick inlaid with patens of bright gold;
> There's not the smallest orb which thou behold'st
> But in his motion like an angel sings,
> Still quiring to the young-eyed cherubims;
> Such harmony is in immortal souls,
> But while this muddy vesture of decay
> Doth grossly close it in we cannot hear it.

From outside and above shines the eternal Divine Light – 'the Light that lighteth every man that cometh into the world'. The light of God is refracted through his creation just as the sunlight falls refracted through the tall stained glass windows.

This concept of the resonance of physical light and the Divine Light was at the heart of the NeoPlatonism of Pseudo Dionysius, a ninth century author whose works were erroneously attributed to a convert of St Paul in the first century and given corresponding authority. They had a profound influence on the philosophy and architecture of the Gothic world. The Divine Light shines through physical things and so affords a ladder up to heaven for the human soul through the contemplation of God's handiwork. When the great Abbot Suger built the Cathedral of St Denis – the French version of Dionysius – just outside Paris he used the newly flowering craft of stained glass to stunning effect. Where cathedrals had before had walls with windows in them they now had windows suspended between a skeleton of stone ribs. In brilliant reds and blues the lives of the saints and the events of Christ's ministry and above all his Cross and Passion were held up for contemplation in jewelled light. When night fell the whole glorious kaleidoscope went blank. Without the Divine Light shining through it the physical world is dumb.

This new riot of colour and carved ornament was deeply offensive to the austere aesthetic of St Bernard. The subaqueous grisaille glass of Salisbury and the strange reserve of its interior which gains its power from the subtle contrasts of dark Purbeck marble and the lighter Chilmark limestone are possibly a deliberate movement away from the rich elaboration of the earlier Gothic buildings. In Salisbury the light floats in the air as if deliberately not drawing attention either to the windows through which it has passed nor to brilliant patches of colour where it falls on the walls or paving. Some churches, particularly the Byzantine churches and the crypts of Romanesque buildings, like St Benoit sur Loire, attain their numinous quality by a mysterious gloom in which the glitter of half-hidden ornaments picks up the light of candles in the darkness. There the numinosity is of enclosure, a sacred cave or womb. Here in Salisbury all is open, candid and transparent. The building has no secrets, except its changing light and austere beauty. Mozart, perhaps, or Haydn, not Beethoven or Brahms.

It is not easy for us living in a post-Enlightenment world with a cosmology and psychology so different from theirs to enter fully into the mind and imagination of our medieval ancestors. In many ways they are closer to St Paul and Plato than we are to them. Neither William Golding nor Edward Rutherford can escape their post-Enlightenment mind-set. Paul takes for granted a cosmology of Principalities and Powers, of angels and archangels, whose unseen influences control and dominate human affairs, often in ways which are oppressive and baneful. He sees himself and his young Christian churches caught up in a cosmic struggle where the main action is taking place in the heavenly realms but spilling over with catastrophic effects into the sublunary world. The coming of Christ and the outpouring of his Spirit is the first beginning of the liberation of humanity from their subjection to the Dominant Powers. The affirmation 'Jesus is Lord' has consequences and implications which are not only personal and political but also strike to the very root of the Heavenly Hierarchies. The lurid imagery of the Book of the Revelation vividly portrays this notion of a cosmic warfare of disordered spiritual Powers.

The reality of angelic powers was thus an universal assumption in the ancient and medieval worlds. Every human institution has its angelic or demonic aspect. When the Seer of the Apocalypse writes to the Seven Churches in Asia he does not address himself to the churchwardens or the elders but the Angel of the Church. 'To the Angel of the Church in Thyatira write...' There is a presiding spirit in the Church there to whom the seer is instructed to address himself.

As twentieth century inhabitants of this planet with a mind-set which is scientific and rationalist it is impossible for us to buy into the cosmological mythology of the ancient world. But before we relegate these mythical images to the dustbin of superstitious fantasy along with unicorns and hydras, we might pause to ask whether these images are a poetical way of describing forces and influences which really do impinge on our human lives but for which we have no ordinary language.

The notion is not so far-fetched. Science has revealed to us that we are constantly being affected in all sorts of intangible and invisible ways by physical forces for which our culture originally had no words. We are also in the grip of social, cultural and psychological forces which mould us in all sorts of unconscious ways. Social psychology and anthropology reveal to us things about ourselves of which we are normally blissfully unaware.

Professor Walter Wink has written a trilogy of thought provoking books suggesting that we should give St Paul and our medieval ancestors the credit for having sufficient grasp on reality not to be pursuing mere chimeras. Men and women in the ancient world were in reality under the dominance of intense social and psychological forces which largely limited and controlled their lives. In that they are no different from ourselves. Our own world is structured and constrained by forces against which we often feel quite powerless. It is a world of multi-layered social systems, individuals and groups which are physically, mentally and spiritually constrained by the values, economics, culture, ethos and unconscious compulsions of their communities and the institutions which compose them. Whole nations are trapped by cultural taboos or economic forces which seem to have a life of their own and to be beyond the control of Government or the multinational corporations which are the chief instruments of the process. The economic and political tides in the affairs of men ebb and flow under the gravitational pull of invisible black holes and even the wisest statesmen have as little chance of stemming them as King Canute. In the twentieth century the 'Powers and Principalities' are the ideologies and '-isms' which sweep through populations and destroy human freedom.

In the 1960s and 70s it was customary to speak of these oppressive structures as 'The System'. Nowhere was the dominance of The System more evident than in South Africa. Apartheid got an implacable hold on the consciousness of a whole nation. It penetrated into the interstices of all institutions, even into the churches; it distorted the vision of otherwise wholesome men and women, poisoning personal and social relationships at their most intimate. It got right inside people's heads. Communism and Fascism did much the same. Carl Jung described as demonic the psychic forces unleashed by the Third Reich. The archetypal energies of the corporate unconscious of the human community influence us for good or ill far more profoundly than we know.

But these are only extreme examples of a much wider phenomenon. Hospitals, schools, factories, all institutions including churches develop a psychic system which sucks groups and individuals into its field of force and moulds their consciousness and perception. It was Karl Marx's contention that market-driven capitalism produces a false consciousness in human beings so deeply rooted that they are unable to envisage any other way of being. We not only introject the basic assumptions of our human institutions and allow them to mould us into a conforming mind and spirit; the *daimon* of the institution has a dynamism of its own. It feeds on the pathology of its members and then uses that psychic energy to coerce them into compliant subservience to its greedy purposes, distorting their perception of reality, eroding their moral freedom and poisoning their social relationships. It is against such hidden forces that the Spirit of God is struggling in defence of human freedom. 'These are the principalities and powers.'

Of course not all systems are toxic or dysfunctional – good families are supportive, nurturing and liberating, so are good schools and good churches. But they are the rare instances of institutions where the *daimon* has been named, confronted and brought into the service of a higher ideal or purpose. It is against this context that we may revisit the teaching of Jesus about the Kingdom of God, which is the central plank of his proclamation. The systems of this world are to become subservient to the system of our God. St John frequently uses the word 'cosmos' – which should perhaps be better translated as 'system' than 'world'. The disciples are in the system, but must not be its slaves. We are not to love the system however seductive it is if it is not God's system.

The Gospel is a direct challenge to all human systems, and they will naturally react to that challenge with rage and violence.

So to return to our Cathedral at last with its strange psychic powers – is its *daimon* an angel and a witch? Angels are always two-faced like Janus. The angel of Light is Lucifer the Dark Lord, the Archangel next to God who wanted to shine not with the glorious transparency of Abbot Suger's windows at St Denis, refracting the Divine Light into the microcosm of the Cathedral, but with his own self-generated radiance. 'Worship me,' he says, 'and I will give you all the Kingdoms of the Earth.' And he can. He really can. But at what a cost – the loss of our true identity, our true perception of reality. In the Book of the Revelation the Seer encounters an Angel and falls at his feet to worship him. Sternly the Angel rebukes him. 'See thou do it not! I am your fellow servant. Worship God alone.' Lucifer offers us absolute rational clarity banishing from the cosmos the Mysterium Tremendum. Our society is well on the way to accepting his offer.

I have sometimes asked friends or visitors what single word they would use to name this Cathedral. Often they have replied almost instantaneously 'Beauty'. That perhaps is the Angel's name. I found a woman in tears at the back of the nave one evening. I sat beside her and asked if I could be of any help. 'No,' she said, 'it's all right. I just didn't know anything could be so beautiful.' So we have named the Angel. Now we must unveil her. Like all great beauties she says, willingly or not, 'Look at me. Give me your heart.'

It is at this point that her ambivalent nature is unveiled. For it was One who had no beauty that we should desire him, no form of human comeliness that said, 'I, if I be lifted up from the earth, will draw the human race to myself'. As the tourists stream in from the ends of the earth out of their coaches through the St Anne's Gate they turn the corner at the north-east angle of the Close and the whole amazing edifice floating on its lawn suddenly confronts them. Stand at that corner for a morning in summer and you will hear as many gasps of astonishment as you may on the brink of the Grand Canyon. 'Look at me,' it says, 'and I will give you your heart's desire.'

The peril of seduction by this white witch is very real. Standing at the doorway, or kneeling in the sanctuary, there must always be a watchman of the Lord, saying over and over again, 'See thou do it not – worship God alone'. The angel must be turned round to face God and point beyond herself so that the building itself becomes transparent to the Transcendent Absolute of the Divine. Clearly some of the 700,000 visitors who drift through the place each year do have that experience. For some people it is life transforming.

In a notably moving lecture Susan Howatch has described her own experience of being seduced – it's her word, not mine – by Salisbury Cathedral soon after coming to live in the Close after a turbulent period in her own personal life:

> I looked out and saw this fantastic sight...the floodlit Cathedral, gorgeous, stunning, out of this world, certainly out of any world I'd been inhabiting. It was radiant, ravishing. I stopped dead and that was the moment when the scales fell from my eyes. I felt I had been presented with some extraordinary gift. I could now see and recognise the overpowering beauty of that Cathedral – which was the sign pointing beyond itself to the reality which was still hidden from my conscious mind.

That experience led to what she calls a monumental upheaval in her spiritual life. Meanwhile, as she continues in her own account,

> I was being systematically seduced by the Cathedral. I used to walk round and round it. Round and round it I walked in all weathers, and after a while it became not so much a building as an animal, something living, something with a personality, something with moods.. More and more mysterious the Cathedral became, and sometimes it was so mysterious it almost seemed eerie. I think eeriness is the shadow side of extreme beauty.

Just for the record I would like to add that most of what I have said was conceived and written before I heard Susan Howatch's Lecture in the Cathedral. It served to confirm what I had already come to understand myself of its beauty and the long shadow it can cast.

So within the building guarding its soul and keeping watch on its angel there must be a community of men and women deeply committed to prayer calling upon the powers of the Holy Spirit to be 'the singing master of its soul', tuning the *daimon* to the purposes of love and holiness. In ways I do not fully understand I believe that the daily Eucharist, the *Opus Dei*, the hours of silence before God of a contemplative people, do open channels for the Spirit of God to inform the human community and all its institutions, and to make them resonate in unconscious ways with the Mysterium Tremendum of the Universe and the archetypal images of the Divine. I want to hold on to an imaginative sense that our medieval ancestors were trying through the medium of their myths and images to articulate spiritual realities which are still part of our own psychic environment, but for which we now have a pitifully inadequate language. I want to suggest that it is possible that from such a platform the Christian Gospel can challenge and address the demonic aspects of the systems of our society in the name of God.

Perhaps we should end where we began. In Stanley Kubrick's beautiful but flawed film *2001 A Space Odyssey* there is one image which has stayed in my mind ever since I first saw it. You may remember that some scientists exploring the surface of the moon discover standing in a remote lunar valley a tall monolithic prism of shiny black basalt or volcanic glass. Clearly it is a sophisticated artefact. But how did it get there? Almost unwillingly it draws them to it. One of them reaches out to touch it and at once it begins to hum. On closer scientific research it turns out that the hum is not generated within the prism but that it is resonating to a beam of radiation generated far out in intergalactic space.

The scientists become haunted by that hum. It feels like a message or a call. Huge resources are mobilised to launch a space ship to track it to its distant origin. But on the journey the ship's immense computer – called George – goes mad and starts to destroy his human crew masters. He is perhaps the *daimon* of the ship. But when finally he has been silenced the ship drifts on through time and space carrying one solitary member of our race to a place of terror, beauty and rebirth where he discovers the beginning and the end of time.

Perhaps in the Christian imagination that is what may happen to those who come in contact with this great edifice of stone.

5

Cathedrals and Christian Scholarship

JOHN MOSES
Provost of Chelmsford

It was at the request of Deans and Provosts that a cathedral was defined in the Care of Cathedrals Measure as 'the seat of the bishop, and a centre of worship and mission'. This definition has been emphatically endorsed in the Report of the Archbishops' Commission on Cathedrals. It leaves no doubt about the place of a cathedral both in the life of a diocese and of the wider community.

It is, however, the words 'the seat of the bishop' which provide the starting point for any discussion of 'Cathedrals and Christian Scholarship'. If the bishop is supremely the one who is required to be the custodian and the interpreter of the tradition; if 'the seat of the bishop' is first and foremost the chair of a teacher; then the relation between the cathedral and the Christian tradition of faith is made explicit in this definition. A cathedral is a cathedral because it has the *cathedra*. No other justification is required for the tradition of godly learning that is still associated in the minds of many people with our English cathedrals.

Cathedrals begin with many advantages. The architecture of our buildings speaks of form, of space, of function, and of transcendence. The liturgy tells of the mysteries of faith and, through the daily offering of worship – and not least of all through the English cathedral tradition of choral worship – it is possible to be drawn into active participation through quiet contemplation and reflection. The priority that is given to music and to all the creative and performing arts speaks of a celebration of life in which there is no separation between the sacred and the secular. The opportunities afforded for teaching the faith are extensive – in public worship, in public lectures and public dialogue, and in the far more informal ways in which people are received and introduced to the cathedral. The tradition of tourism enables people to be in touch with all that cathedrals are able to convey and still to retain their anonymity. There are many who need to enter, to walk around, to look, to sit down, and to be still. Cathedrals are able to respect the private space that we all inhabit in our search for God.

Yes, cathedrals begin with many advantages. The things that have been mentioned are simply the things that come most obviously to mind. People start from many different points, and they travel by many different routes. Where there is imagination and courtesy and vitality, it is possible to introduce them to the Christian tradition which is represented in part by what a cathedral is and in part by what a cathedral does.

The ministry of our cathedrals is one of the unacknowledged success stories of the Church of England in recent decades. It would be possible to point to many places where ancient traditions of worship, of learning, of community, of hospitality, of prophecy have been reinterpreted in the light of contemporary needs. The tradition of godly learning is no exception.

When people in our congregations – in cathedrals and in parish churches – are asked about the priorities of ministry where the interior life of the church is concerned, they will invariably say two things: first, 'Tell us about God'; and secondly, 'Show us how to pray'. Over and above all that has been said about the opportunities provided by architecture, by liturgy, by music, by teaching, by tourism, there will be few cathedrals that have not attempted to address these demands – Tell us about God; Show us how to pray – through theological lectures, through courses of study, through schools of prayer. These activities take different forms, but they are commonplace and they have been built in many instances into the regular life and work of our cathedrals.

It is the French theologian Jean Daniélou who reminds us that, 'The true science of God is that which leads us to love God'.[1] Godly learning lies within the reach of all of us, but cathedrals have been creative in the way they have approached these things. They have proved themselves – like the steward who is trained for the kingdom of heaven – to be well able to bring out of their treasury things old and things new.[2]

But the subject is not 'Cathedrals and Godly Learning'. It is *'Cathedrals and Christian Scholarship'*. Scholarship suggests something more rigorous. It implies research, writing, publication. It suggests contributions to knowledge. It supposes that cathedrals might have a place in the theological enterprise that belongs to the whole church.

Let there be no doubt, however, about the theological enterprise, about the scope of Christian scholarship, about the meaning of Christian theology. One of the significant features of the developing life of the church in the early centuries was the development of a theological tradition that was rational, systematic and apologetic. It was concerned to address the perennial questions concerning God and the world and humankind. It attempted to provide an interpretation of history, a philosophy of history, in the light of which the fundamental search for meaning might be pursued. Its distinguishing characteristics have been from the earliest times a trinitarian faith, an incarnational Christology, and an understanding of redemption through the death and resurrection of Jesus.

Christian theology is concerned to speak about God – His being, His activity, His purposes. It is concerned to reflect upon the world – the richness, the mystery, the meaning of creation. It is concerned to address the questions that have been voiced by men and women over long centuries questions of identity and integrity, of relationships and responsibilities; the fact of evil; the experience of sin and suffering; the search for wholeness.

Christian theology is rooted in the raw material of life. It acknowledges the importance of words, of pictures, of symbols. It takes seriously the life-stories of individuals and of communities. It takes account of the paradoxes of experience.

It is the task of theology to speak about God. It is the task of Christian theology to speak about the God and Father of our Lord Jesus Christ. Theology is informed and enlarged and tested by other disciplines. It cannot do its work in isolation. There is a comprehensiveness and a totality about Christian theology which require it to interpret all knowledge and experience in the light of the cross. It remains for those who seek understanding through faith the primary discipline of coherence and interpretation because it finds in God the principle of unity that holds all things in being

But what is it all for? Where does it all lead? Is there some simple way in which all that Christian theology is feeling after might be expressed? Let the answer be expressed in these words. There is an urgent need to attempt from the standpoint of Christian faith a comprehensive and systematic understanding of the world. If religion has been disowned and disregarded by recent generations, and especially in the western world, it is at least in part because it is no longer seen to relate to people's experience of life and to illuminate it. But if it is possible to interpret our world aright, wrestling with the Christian tradition in the light of contemporary knowledge, then it might be possible to recover for Christian theology its ancient claim to be the discipline of coherence because it speaks of the God who holds within himself the whole of being.

If it is right to suggest that these are the areas of concern that properly come within the meaning of Christian theology, within the scope of Christian scholarship, then the question has to be asked, Why should there be a place for cathedrals in this theological enterprise that manifestly belongs to the whole church? And more than that, Has it not been the case over the centuries that the church – and I speak specifically of the Church of England – has been able to look to the universities and their faculties or departments of divinity or theology to ensure that the theological tradition is maintained and renewed?

Yes, there are questions to be addressed, but the prior question can be expressed in this way, *Where does the church do its theology?* There is always the temptation for the church to withdraw into its own interior life. But the church is required to live in an open relationship with society, and theology has traditionally been explored and developed in dialogue with other disciplines within the wider community of learning.

It would be absurd to suggest that theology can only be done in cathedrals. But it is entirely appropriate to suggest that cathedrals are amongst the places where theology can and should be done in *partnership with others.*

There can be no doubt that the church has opportunities today which it has not previously enjoyed with regard to our universities if it wishes to enter into collaborative arrangements which will make provision for theological research and teaching and writing. But this is not to say that the church can continue to rely upon our universities to provide unaided the development of a Christian theological tradition. Let full account be taken in the first instance of what is happening to our universities and of the constraints within which they are required to work.

There is still in the minds of many an idea of the university as a community of learning which is able to provide its students with an initiation into the traditions, the culture, the thought-forms, the intellectual discoveries of a civilization. Cardinal Newman's idea of a university as a School of Universal Learning is one that has never been completely abandoned, although it has changed in significant respects. The university still remains, ideally, a human community, a community of learning, that draws together teachers and pupils in many spheres of knowledge. It is a place of thought where ideas can circulate freely and be tested. It is a cooperative enterprise in which different minds, critical of each other, can engage in a common process.

Those involved in our universities are now having to deal with the implications of major changes in society: a declining eighteen-year-old population; the shifting emphasis from regarding higher education as a once-in-a-lifetime experience to continuing education; the need to provide access to higher education for women, for those from low-income groups, for ethnic minority groups, and for mature students; the changing pattern of employment with the movement towards high technology and the service industries; the impact of information technology; the pressures on public expenditure.

Universities are not comfortable places at the present time. Changes are taking place at an accelerating pace and they are changing the nature of the university community; changing, perhaps, even the idea of a university itself. Change must never be rejected out of hand. Some developments can properly be welcomed. But, to impose a different purpose on a university is to change its character. It is not difficult to understand why those who are deeply involved in the life of our universities as teachers and administrators feel that they are entering a world where inappropriate pressures are being brought to bear upon long-established traditions of independence and scholarship.

Excellence has been the traditional hallmark of a university. Efficiency could well be the touchstone of the new settlement in higher education. The level of public funding is declining with the consequence that new sources of funding are required. There is a new emphasis on vocational training for work in a technological society. There is some desire that universities should become more regionally centred and should enter into a new partnership with their immediate environment. There will be an increasing emphasis on continuing education. Academic staff will almost certainly find that security of tenure can no longer be taken for granted.

It is not surprising that many subjects that have long since been established within the national pattern of university education should feel very vulnerable in this brave new world. It will not be easy to demonstrate why they should be maintained at all costs in an environment that is increasingly scientific, vocational and competitive. Theology is no exception. The fact that Christian theology has been there from the beginning in the universities of Western Europe, that it was a prime mover in the establishment of the most ancient and prestigious centres of learning, that it has occupied a position of pre-eminence throughout long centuries, will not provide any security for the future.

None of our theological faculties or departments is exempt. There is no shortage of applicants for degree courses in theology, but established teaching posts are being abandoned or suspended in some places as vacancies occur. Departments that survive in a diminished form are having to revise their syllabuses to take account of the reduction of teaching staff; academics are under increasing pressure to provide evidence of their productivity by their teaching, their research and their publications. Further cuts may occur if universities are required to give stronger emphasis to scientific and technological subjects. It is not always easy to argue the case for *Christian* theology in a secular society. It will certainly be judged more important in some places to give priority to courses of study that take seriously the inter-faith dialogue that must take place in a multi-faith society.

Can it be demonstrated that a comprehensive and coherent vision of reality will always escape us unless Christian theology is able to make its distinctive contribution to these schools of universal learning that must now adapt to meet the national demand to be skilled, to compete, to survive? Does Christian theology have some claim upon the limited resources for which all university departments must compete because it has a unique contribution to make to our understanding of humankind and of society?

Christian theology is required to answer these questions and to do so in a pluralist and secular society. The institutions, the rituals, the patterns of Christian faith and practice have lost their once unquestioned recognition and significance. Theological insight, religious experience and practice, have become peripheral – or appear to have become peripheral – to the needs and concerns of large numbers of people. Yet those who profess no faith are bound to concede at the very least that religion continues to be a vital element in human experience, that Christian values have shaped western civilization, providing the basis of government and law, of personal and social ethics, and influencing all forms of artistic endeavour. An ideal university will not be dominated either by theological considerations, or by utilitarian or professional studies. But a university which makes no provision for the study of theology might be judged to be providing a pattern of education that is grievously inadequate.

Theology rests its case in large measure upon the conviction that truth is essentially complex and mysterious. It proceeds from the ancient principle of faith seeking understanding. The theological understanding holds that the search for God and the search for truth are inseparable from and need each other. The theological understanding holds that a rediscovery of the connection between faith and thought can serve the respective needs of theology, of the university and the modern world.

It would be untrue to suggest, however, that the plight of theology in our universities is being received by the Church with any great degree of apprehension. The churches have struggled hard to maintain a wide range of sector ministries, and not least of all through the provision of pastoral chaplaincies in places of higher education. But the churches are preoccupied, in large measure, with their own domestic concerns: the payment and deployment of their clergy and the maintenance of inherited patterns of ministry. There is a good deal of investment in resourcing parishes and deaneries through the establishment of diocesan councils and diocesan officers with special responsibility for different aspects of the church's ministry. There are strong pressures that focus any theological reflection upon the issues that are immediately to hand: the local, the practical, the contemporary.

These pressures, although appropriate, can be seductive if they lead to the conclusion that it is possible to dispense with the rigorous theological critique that so many complex issues require. It is easy to caricature the theology that has been done in our universities as esoteric, élitist, expensive and unrelated to the affairs of the church or the world. It is less easy to accept at face value the misgivings that are to be found within the Church from time to time concerning the objective, rational, critical approach that is adopted in university faculties and departments of theology. These misgivings are compounded in some places by a suspicion of theological liberalism or theological radicalism. But a church that takes the theological enterprise seriously will also view with very great concern the resurgence of a theological fundamentalism within the church which refuses to address the questions with which people are actually wrestling day by day.

If this analysis of what is happening in our universities and in the church is fundamentally correct, why does it follow that there should be for our cathedrals a special responsibility to embrace as one of their primary concerns a commitment to Christian theology and Christian scholarship? Could it be that there are in the very nature of our cathedrals certain things which should enable them to be well qualified to take this commitment?

First, there is a tradition of independence which has been well used by cathedrals in many places to pioneer new patterns of ministry. It is this tradition of independence – if it is used aright – which can be so precious. Christian theology and Christian scholarship demand absolute honesty, even – in the best sense – free thinking. The traditional emphasis within the Church of England upon scripture, tradition and reason acknowledges a commitment to the fundamental principles of catholicism and reformation. It is not comprehensiveness but comprehension, not liberalism but liberality, that

are the authentic marks of the English tradition. The independence of cathedrals – properly interpreted – could ensure
that they bring to the theological enterprise the best traditions of independent thought, of critical enquiry.

Secondly, cathedral foundations are corporate bodies.
To a far greater extent than might be found anywhere else in
the church, cathedral chapters are required to bring together
a range of disciplines and skills. The theologian, the liturgist,
the teacher, the musician, the pastor, the administrator, the
entrepreneur, are required to live together day by day within
the framework of a collegiate life with a corporate responsibility for the institution. Let the point be made again. Theology cannot do its work in isolation. It will be informed and
enlarged and tested by other disciplines. Christian theology is
therefore required to be multidisciplinary. The corporate life
of our cathedrals, the corporate nature of the responsibilities
we share, can serve to remind us of the interdisciplinary, the
multi-disciplinary, approach that properly belongs to Christian theology and Christian scholarship.

Thirdly, cathedrals understand the true meaning of
establishment. They know what it is to be a community
church; to operate on the boundaries of church and community life; to be a church – in Archbishop William Temple's
notable words – that exists for the sake of those who do not
belong. The network of relationships within which every
English cathedral is inescapably caught up has much to say
about the expectations and the opportunities that surround
us in the work of ministry. Cathedrals are required to be in
dialogue with a large number of institutions and individuals.
Dialogue has always been at the heart of the theological tradition: the dialogue between faith and reason, between scripture and tradition, between nature and grace. There is
something here that will also come to the aid of cathedrals if
they choose to engage seriously with the demands of Christian theology, of Christian scholarship.

Fourthly, cathedrals understand folk religion. Cathedrals embody the religious tradition. They are required time
and again to give expression to the religious aspirations of

those who come. But they understand the different degrees of association, of commitment, that people want and are capable of sustaining. Cathedrals are well placed to interpret the inarticulate religion of those who cannot embrace without qualification the assumptions and commitments of discipleship. The church is suspicious of folk religion. Its distinctive theological traditions – catholic, evangelical and liberal – have not always found it easy to come to terms with folk religion. Alan Wilkinson's reflections on the failure of the Church of England to respond adequately to the theological and the moral questions posed by the Great War of 1914 to 1918 included an acknowledgement that the Church had failed also to understand the expressions of folk religion because 'its evangelicalism was too puritan, biblicist and pietistic; its liberalism too detached and academic; its catholicism too selfconscious, dogmatic and nostalgic'.[3] Those who have responsibility for public ministry are bound to be mindful of the emptiness of a vague Christianity that attaches no vital importance to sin, to grace, to redemption, or to the church as a divine community. But let it be acknowledged that folk religion contains within itself some acknowledgement of the religious dimension and seeks expression from time to time of that search for meaning that lies at the heart of all theological endeavour.

All that has been suggested is that cathedrals are amongst the places where theology can and should be done. If there is within our cathedrals a desire to develop the traditions not only of godly learning but of Christian scholarship, then it may well be found that they are greatly assisted by their traditions of independence and of corporate responsibility, by their understanding of establishment and of folk religion. The tradition of independence speaks of freedom of thought. The tradition of corporate responsibility speaks of an approach that is interdisciplinary, multi-disciplinary. The understanding of establishment speaks of the necessity of dialogue. The understanding of folk religion speaks of the search for meaning.

It is bound to be the case that scholarship – in the sense

of research and writing and publication – will be done by individuals. Scholarship is the work of scholars. Cathedrals are very busy places – at times frenetically busy; but they are institutions where the *opus dei* provides – ideally – not merely the boundaries but the rhythm of life. The question is, therefore, whether it is possible to build into the rhythm of the life of our cathedrals sufficient space for those who are able to do so to pursue their theological work.

There can be no doubt that the work of Christian scholarship must still be pursued in large measure in our universities. Some of our bishops will ensure that they find the time to read and think and write. It would be good to think that there might be a rediscovery of the Anglican tradition which has witnessed over the generations a long line of clergy who as incumbents in the Church of England have contributed by their learning to the intellectual life of the church and of society. But it may well be in our cathedrals – because of the nature of the institution and because of the opportunities they can provide – that the tradition of godly learning, the work of Christian scholarship, might properly be taken up and developed.

But this subject suggests another question. It is not merely whether cathedral clergy *as individuals* can be set free to engage in the theological enterprise. It is also whether cathedrals *as institutions* can pursue in partnership with the universities the work of Christian scholarship. Certainly the experience of one cathedral – Chelmsford – over recent years provides evidence of two initiatives which say something about the way in which Cathedrals as institutions can work.

First, there is the the relationship that Chelmsford Cathedral has established with Essex University. It is now more than eight years since a Centre for the Study of Theology was established in that university. It came out of extensive discussions over a long period with the bishop, with the vice-chancellor and the registrar at the university, with the cathedral chapter, and with the Anglican chaplaincy of the university. The initiative rested from the beginning with the cathedral chapter and the university Anglican chaplaincy.

Indeed, the Centre has been sponsored throughout the last eight years by the chapter and the chaplaincy. Monies have been provided by the bishop and the chapter so that the work of the Centre can be secured during these early years. Rooms have been made available by the university; and all the interested parties have entered into commitments which have made it possible for the Centre to promote units of teaching within the university's programme of continuing education, together with theological research and publication.

The role of the two sponsoring bodies deserves some closer examination. Chelmsford Cathedral – in common with many other cathedrals – has attempted to find new ways in recent years of developing the study of academic and applied theology. No two cathedrals are the same, but there is a general awareness that our cathedrals are community churches. What this means in practice is that they will value their working relationships with other institutions within their localities, that they will work hard to identify the aspirations of the community, and that they will attempt to make their facilities and resources available for education. If a cathedral is a cathedral because it has the *cathedra*, then no other justification is required for the special claim that theology must always have upon the resources of our cathedrals. And a cathedral, if it proceeds with courtesy and commitment, is able to bring together interested parties, to pursue discussions and possibilities, to provide an external validation, and to enter into long-term commitments.

But no initiative on the part of the cathedral chapter could have succeeded without the imaginative work that had been done over the previous years by the Anglican chaplaincy at the university in pioneering a programme of adult educational work. University chaplaincies will be mindful of the needs of the whole institution. The pastoral work of the chaplain will have a primary claim upon his time and energy. But the nature and purpose of the university demand that the chaplain should provide some opportunity for those who are seeking to explore the truth of the Christian faith. The weekly seminar programme that had been provided by the Anglican chaplaincy over several years had established a sizeable constituency of support, drawing large numbers of people from outside the university. A university which was taking seriously its programme of continuing education recognised the contribution that the chaplaincy might make. The initiative that was taken by the cathedral chapter in arguing the case for the Centre, and the solid work that had been done by the chaplaincy, encouraged the university to respond positively and to enter into a working relationship which the university, the cathedral and the chaplaincy believe to be to their mutual advantage.

The Centre has been granted a unique status. It is *in* but not *of* the university. It has chosen to work from the beginning on an interdisciplinary basis in the broad field of theology and society. It takes no part whatsoever in first degree work, although serious consideration is now being given to the establishment of a Master's Degree in Theology and Society. But through its seminar programmes, its public lectures, and the collaborative work of its Fellows, the Centre has secured a place for theological teaching and research and publication in a university which since its foundation over thirty years ago has prided itself on what at times could only be called a selfconscious and strident secularism.

Secondly, it might be helpful to turn to the relationship that Chelmsford Cathedral is establishing with one of the nation's youngest universities, the Anglia Polytechnic University. Anglia is a regional university. It encompasses a large number of affiliated institutions of higher education. Its two main campuses are in Chelmsford and Cambridge, and it so happens that the Chelmsford campus falls entirely within the cathedral parish. The cathedral has enjoyed the closest relationship with the university as it has made the transition – in common with many other institutions – from being a college of higher education, a polytechnic, and now – only within the last three years – a university.

The Anglia Polytechnic University is a very good instance of what was meant earlier when reference was made to the network of institutions within which every cathedral is inescapably caught up. But little could have been attempted without the desire on both sides – the university and the cathedral – to enter into a close working relationship with each other. This relationship has been strengthened and developed not merely by the use that the university is able to make of the cathedral from time to time, but by the appointment of the Provost as the Rector of the university, by the appointment of a full-time Anglican chaplain who is also an honorary associate chaplain of the cathedral, and by the establishment of a Cathedral Choral Foundation which will look to students at the university for its choral scholars.

What is so exciting, however, at the present time is the possibility of a Master's degree in Pastoral Theology which the cathedral is negotiating with the university. It is still early days, but here again is an instance of how initiatives can be taken and opportunities for serious theological work opened up. There are serious questions to be asked concerning resources – time, library facilities, and the availability of a sufficient number of people from outside the university who are competent to teach theology at Master's degree level. But if these matters can be resolved satisfactorily, what will have been secured will be the opportunity for clergy and lay people, but especially clergy, from all over the diocese to pursue academic and applied theology – Pastoral Theology – in the context of an open relationship between the cathedral and the university.

These two instances – the Centre for the Study of Theology at Essex University and the serious possibility of a Master's degree in Pastoral Theology at the Anglia Polytechnic University – serve to indicate the ways in which cathedrals as institutions can take forward the work of Christian scholarship. There are many developments within higher education at the present time which raise serious questions about what is happening to our universities; but there is also an awareness today that universities belong to their local communities, that continuing education must have a high priority, and that working relationships can be established with institutions that take seriously their own integrity – academically and professionally. It may well be that what can be said out of the experience of one cathedral can be matched in other places. What cannot be in dispute is that the opportunities exist for cathedrals to take forward the work of theological education, of Christian scholarship, in collaboration with our universities, if they have the desire to do so.

It is nonetheless true that any significant movement in the direction of theological education, of Christian scholarship, requires a serious investment on the part of cathedrals. There must obviously be a commitment to theology as the church's primary discipline. There must also be a desire to work in collaboration with institutions of higher education. There must be a rediscovery of the office of a canon chancellor or a canon theologian. One person must carry within chapter the primary responsibility for the development of the cathedral's work in this area. Theology, like liturgy, manifestly belongs to the whole church, and cannot be easily located in any synodical body. Cathedrals are well able to carry for the bishop and for the church in the diocese the church's public commitment to these areas of primary concern. There must inevitably be questions also concerning funding. No major developments in ministry are easily attempted in any of our cathedrals without some diversion of resources. But where these things exist – a commitment to theology as the church's primary discipline; a willingness to work in collaboration with our universities; a development of the office of the canon chancellor or the canon theologian; and the releasing of the necessary financial resources – then it is possible for our cathedrals to address in small but significant ways some of the opportunities that undoubtedly exist for taking forward the work of Christian scholarship.

Cathedrals begin with many advantages. There is a tradition of godly learning that is still associated in the minds of many people with our English cathedrals. Christian *scholarship* takes this further and asks for something more searching. The continuing rediscovery of a theological tradition that is rational, systematic and apologetic belongs to the whole church. But cathedrals might yet be thought to have a place within the theological enterprise and a significant contribution to make. There is an urgent need to attempt from the standpoint of Christian faith a comprehensive and systematic understanding of the world. It is only possible to proceed in the light of the ancient principle of faith seeking understanding. To work at the discovery of who God is, and what God is doing, and what God requires of his people, is one of the most sensitive and enriching activities in which Christian people engage. The limited experience of our cathedrals over recent years suggests that it is possible to do this in collaboration with others because within the ordered and flexible framework of our corporate life there is a desire to make explicit our commitment to theology as our primary resource.

NOTES

1. Jean Daniélou, *God and Us*, Trans. by Walter Roberts, Mowbray 1957, p.171.
2. St Matthew 13 52.
3. Alan Wilkinson, *The Church of England and the First World War*, SPCK 1978, p.196.

6

Cathedrals and God's Word of Life

JOHN ARNOLD
The Dean of Durham

The Gospel according to St Luke, chapter 18, verses 9-14:

> Jesus told this parable to some who trusted in themselves that
> they were righteous and despised others. Two men went up to
> the Temple to pray, one a Pharisee and the other a tax collec-
> tor. The Pharisee standing by himself was praying thus, 'God,
> I thank you that I am not like other people: thieves, rogues,
> adulterers or even like this tax collector. I fast twice a week, I
> give a tenth of all my income.' But the tax collector standing
> far off would not even look up to heaven but was beating his
> breast and saying, 'God, be merciful to me, a sinner '.

This is just to set the scene in the Temple for what I want to
say about Cathedrals, which Richard Hooker taught us to
regard as temples of the living God: but I take as my text an
old Punch cartoon, that splendid full-page Du Maurier picture from the first decade of this century, showing a young
Edwardian beauty with hour-glass figure reclining upon a
chaise longue and receiving a visit from a very proper young
curate in full morning dress, his top hat, stick and gloves set
out on a stool beside him. He is leaning forward and asking
her earnestly: My dear, would you rather be beautiful or
good? And she, gazing back at him in sultry fashion through

heavy-lidded eyes, is murmuring: I would rather be beautiful and repent.

In cathedrals we have no choice. We can only be beautiful – and repent. I do not need to speak to you of beauty – the stone, the wood, the glass and iron, the flowers, the setting, the music, all speak for themselves: and we thank all those living and departed who have contributed to these many delights. It is however worth pausing to note that the very fact that we take the alliance of beauty and worship for granted in cathedrals has been bought at a great price. If the Empress Irene II – a battle-axe of the first water even by Byzantine standards – had not won the iconoclastic controversy with blood and tears, if the Anglicans led by Richard Hooker had not defeated the Puritans in the interpretation of the Elizabethan settlement, if Church and King and Bishop Cosin and the Book of Common Prayer had not been restored after the Commonwealth, we would of course still be worshipping God, but in bare buildings with maimed rites and plain notes if any. But we would be doing so, therefore, with a diminished view of Almighty God, Father, free, loving, creative, sovereign, spontaneous and joyful, and of His Son who came to raise our human nature by adoption and grace to the level of his own likeness, and or the Holy and life-giving Spirit, through whom the love of God is shed abroad in our hearts. Cathedrals exist to keep open a large view of God and of His goodness and a large view of human potentiality as well as a realistic view of human sinfulness. That is why my two themes are beauty and repentance.

And we have plenty to repent of. We must have, or the General Synod would not have passed the Care of Cathedrals Measure of 1990 with its alarming penalties and insulting implications; and the Archbishops would not have set up a Commission to inquire into all aspects of Cathedral life, especially their governance. We must have, or we would not be continually compared disparagingly with parish churches, rather quaintly and indeed acrobatically described as simultaneously the backbone and the front line and the glory of the Church of England. There is only one glory of the Church of

England and that is neither its parish churches nor its cathedrals – it is the transmission of the Gospel, the scandal of the crucifixion, the preaching of the Cross of Christ. It is by that comparison alone, in the light of and at the foot of the cross that we have much – indeed everything – to repent of.

And Cathedrals, which offer us so much temptation, like the Scribes and Pharisees, to enjoy greetings in the market place and the best seats in the synagogue, also offer us the opportunity simply to follow the Publican and go to the temple to pray and give up trying to make ourselves acceptable by our works to God or man, to commissions or committees, to all the people who write in with their complaints – a tiny proportion, it is true, of those who write appreciatively, but still to be heeded – to give up pretending, to give up trying to justify ourselves and to substitute justification by works for justification by faith and justification by self for justification by God. I answer every letter I receive, painstakingly explaining what we do and why we do it, apologizing when we are in the wrong, pushing back when it seems to me that we are in the right. But often because I know that I and my colleagues and the whole system of religion by which we are trammelled are so deeply corrupted by sin, I just want to drop my pen or close my lips, and only open them to say, 'God have mercy on me a sinner'. And then I realise that I cannot even do that, because in Cathedrals we pay other people to sing these words for us, hauntingly and agonizingly beautifully, so that the meaning is simultaneously obscured and enhanced, *Kyrie eleison, Christe eleison, Kyrie eleison.*

Cathedrals are places for experiencing deeply the all-embracing corruption of sin and – even more deeply – the all-embracing scope and grandeur of the love of God. A Russian Orthodox priest, drawing heavily on his knowledge of Byzantium, said to me when he learned that I was Dean of an English cathedral (Rochester then, not Durham): Father John, where there is very great beauty there is always very great wickedness. That is true, and one of the reasons why it is true is that some people give themselves to the cult of the beauty of inanimate objects not as a means of enhancing their love of God and neighbour but as a substitute for them. And that is idolatry. A year after the 400th anniversary of the birth of George Herbert I quote:

> A man that looks on glass
> On it may stay his eye
> Or, if he pleaseth, through it pass
> And there the heaven espy.

It is precisely because of the magnitude of temptation and the certainty of falling that cathedrals which are places of such great wickedness must also be places given over to forgiveness. When Michael Turnbull, now Bishop of Durham, joined us at Rochester as a canon, after being Archbishop's chaplain and parish priest and university chaplain and Chief Secretary of the Church Army, he said to me: 'Now in middle life I have rediscovered grace. Everywhere else I was expected to take the lead, to achieve something, to work wonders. Here I step onto a moving travellator of matins and evensong and the faith which I need, I do not have to make for myself. It is the faith of the Church.'

Now listen to another voice: 'Lara was not religious... she did not believe in ritual.' That's not me, that's Boris Pasternak in his masterpiece *Doctor Zhivago*. Lara was not religious ... she did not believe in ritual; but sometimes, to enable her to bear her life she needed the accompaniment of an inward music and she could not always compose it for herself. That music was God's word of life and it was to weep over it that she went to church. Once at the beginning of December ... she went to pray with such a heavy heart that she felt as if at any moment the earth might open at her feet and the vaulted ceiling of the church cave in... In the time it took her to make her way past the worshippers, buy two candles and find her place, the deacon had rattled off the nine Beatitudes at a pace suggesting that they were quite well enough known without his help. Blessed are the poor in spirit ...Blessed are they that mourn... Blessed are they that hunger and thirst after righteousness...

Lara trembled and stood still. This was for her. He was

saying: Happy are the downtrodden. There is after all something to be said for them. They have everything before them. That was what Christ thought. That was His opinion. That's magical, isn't it? Only a great poet could have written that as the best expression I know in prose of what can happen in cathedrals, where wounded souls can slip in, feeling like death, and hide behind the pillars and listen to someone else singing the liturgy and be touched by God's word of life and be broken down and lifted up in one and the same movement, and know that they count, that they are a child of God, worth far more than any sparrow. Pasternak, who was a great sinner as well as a great poet, not very brave, not very faithful, was preserved by God alone of all the poets of the Russian silver age, who perished everyone in the great terror or the war, he was preserved to write that, to say what God's grace can do for the teenage mistress or a middle-aged roué; and he could say it because he knew what it could do for him. It can do the same for us and for our cathedrals and for all who come to them, seeking beauty, which they know they are seeking, and repentance, which they may not know they are seeking until they hear the music or God's word of life, which they cannot compose for themselves – and now at last realise that they do not need to, because both repentance and forgiveness are free gifts, pure grace.

The form in which God's word of life came to Lara was the chanting of the Beatitudes – Blessed are the poor in spirit, blessed are they that mourn, blessed are they that hunger and thirst after righteousness – but it could have come through glass, or painting, through sculpture or embroidery or simply through the building itself.

And I want to insist that it is the cathedral itself – the cathedral in its wholeness and integrity – which is our main concern and something greater than any of its parts or the sum of its parts. I shall go on to speak of individual works of art which contribute to the cathedral and which are enhanced by being set in a cathedral – but it is the Cathedral itself which is primary and which it is our task to maintain. For cathedrals witness, in an age of fragmentation and specialisation, of analysis rather than synthesis, of division rather than cohesion, to a unity of purpose and a harmony of many different voices which can convey wholeness and healing to a generation which needs these things above all else. These great buildings by their size and magnanimity and by the regular offering of worship, can give shape to God's two great gifts of space and time for people who in their everyday lives never have enough of either, because they perceive them as formless and of no worth. Cathedrals speak freely of the spaciousness and generosity of God in creation as well as of the continuity of the church and the creativity of men and women through the ages, including our own. This is one reason why entry to cathedrals should, if possible, be free. Entry into the building should be an experience, not a transaction; and all the English cathedrals now give great care to welcoming visitors and helping them appreciate what they find. It is a fine art to make available sufficient explanatory material while still leaving enough unspoken, so that visitors are given the opportunity to have their own experiences of transcendence, rather than have second-hand experiences thrust upon them. As a rule, we only let our own people act as guides – members of the Foundation or of our own congregation who know the building as a place of worship first and as a cultural monument second. In all that we do, we seek to help tourists become pilgrims, because we know that pilgrimage is a fine and enlarging human experience while tourism can be narrow and alienating.

Pilgrimages grew up because of the association of saints and sanctity with particular places; and it has always been a task for the church to lead pilgrims on from an interest in physical objects to the personal and spiritual associations which they bear. All the great English medieval shrines were destroyed in 1547; but their sites have remained known and hallowed and they are not only increasingly appreciated today, but are even being added to. Canterbury, for example, the scene of the martyrdom of Thomas Becket, now houses in its Corona a notable Chapel to the martyrs of the twentieth century. Rochester was the Bishopric both of John Fisher

(d. 1535) and of Nicholas Ridley (d.1555), who died for their faith and for conscience's sake though on different sides at the time of the Reformation. The double cult of these martyrs is an inspiration to us now in the ecumenical perspectives of the late twentieth century. Many people visit Rochester Cathedral because it is the church which Charles Dickens – now I believe the most popular author in the world – knew and loved; and other cathedrals have their own literary and secular saints. The continual re-telling of heroic tales and the preservation of the corporate memory of society through annual commemorations is part of the rhythm of cathedral life and a contribution to the culture of the nation.

The need of visitors and tourists to understand their experience and re-live it must be met by the provision of worthy guide books and souvenirs. This is a complex area, because many of our cathedrals need substantial income from gift stalls and shops in order to maintain their fabric and ministry. Remember that there is no church tax in England and only recently has there been any state aid for cathedrals. But commercial considerations cannot be the only criteria; and cathedrals, which accept their vocation to maintain the highest standards in every other sphere, should also be seeking to educate public taste, when it comes to marketing souvenirs, not just to profit from it. Those who have debased the sensibilities of the faithful by feeding them on *kitsch* will have something to answer for at the Day of Judgment.

Schools are increasingly coming to appreciate the educational value of visits to cathedrals; and many of our English Cathedrals now have a very happy experience of co-operating with the education authorities in producing workpacks and study-sheets, geared to the needs of different age groups. We also produce our own audio-visual programmes and provide scripts for professional productions. The past few years have seen a move away from mainly art-historical descriptions to bolder attempts to penetrate the mystery of these great buildings and to expose the faith of those who built them and of those who still worship in them. Educational material of this kind may properly be called evangelistic, for it prepares the mind to receive the great realities which produced and still produce Christian faith – creation, incarnation, redemption, the forgiveness of sins and the hope of glory.

So can exhibitions, which can take many forms, depending on the history and the possessions of particular places as well as on the availability of suitable rooms. Permanent exhibitions have traditionally displayed the treasures of cathedrals. Again, it is worth recalling how much of the wealth of the medieval Ecclesia Anglicana was lost or dispersed not only during the Reformation in the sixteenth century but also during the Civil War in the mid-seventeenth century. Few of our Cathedrals can rival the great treasuries of Europe; but this may be no bad thing, as conventional displays of large amounts of gold and silver in churches have become problematical in an age which now questions this kind of wealth in the name of the Gospel. Security and insurance are expensive and it is pointless simply to lock everything away in bank vaults. In Rochester, where we were fortunate enough to possess very fine silver plate, we found a compromise solution by loaning the collection to the city museum nearby for permanent display and retrieving it for use on major festivals. Many cathedrals, however, help the churches of their dioceses, just as our city helped us , by providing secure spaces for the exhibition of treasures from the parishes. In this way, proper honour is done to the skills of artists and craftsmen, much local history is preserved in the locality; and parishioners can enjoy after only a short journey things which after all belong to them and which they ought not to have to go to London to see.

In recent years cathedrals have also been developing explanatory exhibitions of their own history and of the history of their cities. An age which has witnessed the loss of so much of its heritage through war, development and neglect, looks to cathedrals as previous ages looked to monasteries and abbeys to preserve at least a remnant of its culture.

Apart from permanent exhibitions, cathedrals are increasingly staging temporary exhibitions which may be of works by celebrated contemporary artists or by local school-children; they may be displays by missionary societies or other church agencies; they may set out dramatically some of the great issues of the day such as war and peace, hunger and plenty, human rights and deprivation. Whatever they are, their promoters feel that in some way, which is difficult to specify, their message is enhanced by the setting of the cathedral, which in this sense acts as a loud speaker for them. English cathedrals are becoming more adventurous in the range of topics thought suitable for exhibition in a cathedral; they are returning to that open-hearted acceptance of concern for the whole of human life which characterised the high Middle Ages at their best. Certainly, we find that our 900-year-old Romanesque Cathedral has a more robust and less fragile atmosphere than many more modern parish churches. The sense of the sacred re-asserts itself with effortless ease which gives us the courage to welcome the so-called secular, as in a recent celebration of the Eucharist with music by the great jazz composer and player, Duke Ellington, and the more controversial exhibiting of the AIDS quilt.

We may have been led astray by our consciousness of the sheer durability of much which we have received from the past into assuming that permanence is a necessary quality of all art and culture. But cathedrals – because of their intrinsic sense of antiquity and permanence – make excellent settings for the impermanent, the transitory and the ephemeral. Perhaps the most notable example of this in England – so everyday that we take it for granted and scarcely reckon it to be culture – is flower-arranging. Every week (except in penitential seasons) the most wonderful displays are created by enthusiastic amateurs, only to fade and be replaced by yet more wonderful displays in which art and nature are skillfully allied to the glory of God and the delight of His children.

English cathedrals, as well as being houses of prayer and temples of the living God, have also always been places of sacred learning and schools of sacred song. They maintain libraries – not only as collections of ancient books, incunabula, manuscripts and archives – but also as working libraries, purchasing new works and keeping up-to-date as centres of study for the clergy and laity of their dioceses. Some, like Canterbury, Winchester and Durham are among the great libraries of the land; others like Hereford maintain the old furnishings and even the chained books of an earlier age; yet others like Salisbury and Lincoln with their copies of Magna Carta preserve *in situ* the written monuments not only of our history but also of our laws and liberties. All welcome scholars and researchers, mainly in history and theology, though in earlier ages cathedrals contributed more than their share to the development of the natural sciences too. I have spoken of the damage done to some aspects of our heritage at the Reformation, which in England took an iconoclastic form from which Lutheranism was largely spared. It is only fair to add that it was the Reformation which gave a great impetus to literacy in England and cathedral libraries are one of the best witnesses to the impact of printing, of book production and the rise of modern critical scholarship in the life of our Church and nation. They remain places in which books are still read and even, by the grace of God and despite much busy-ness, written.

But books are not the first thing which come into our minds when we hear the word 'cathedral'. Almost certainly our first thought will be music, for our cathedrals preserve the tradition of daily sung services – some both morning and evening – though most now only at Evensong, with Choral Matins and Sung Eucharist also on Sundays only. The typical English cathedral choirs consist of boys singing treble and grown men singing alto, tenor and bass. They have a unique sound, quite different from choirs of men and women. They preserve a repertoire of more than a thousand pieces from the thirteenth century to the present day, with something of a bias towards the English church music of the late sixteenth and early seventeenth centuries and the revived musical tradition of the nineteenth century. Daily practice enables young choristers from the age of 8 not only to sing complex music confidently, but also to sing the psalms meditatively and prayerfully to Anglican chant, the psalter remaining as always at the heart of the daily office.

Cathedral choirs have been remarkably flexible in coping with changes in the liturgy, for *The Alternative Service Book 1980* allows and even encourages the maintenance of the classical heritage of church music. Roman Catholics come to our cathedrals now in order to hear the masses of Byrd and Palestrina sung in Latin. It is a strange fact that the Church of England, with its comparatively restricted resources, sustains much of the professional musical life of the nation; indeed, it is said that the largest permanent professional choir in England is the choir of St Paul's Cathedral. We face many problems, not least criticism from within the church, in maintaining the music of our cathedrals. Changes in the nature of our schools may make it more difficult to recruit and train choristers, but still, this is a golden age of church music. Standards have never been higher and, through recordings and the broadcast twice a week on the BBC of Choral Evensong and other church music, more and more people are coming to appreciate this part of our heritage.

It goes without saying that the traditional instrument both for accompaniment and for recitals is the organ, but a welcome feature of recent years has been the growth in the use of a wider range of instruments, though full orchestral masses remain a comparative rarity.

Apart from maintaining their own tradition, cathedrals also serve as centres for the musical life of their dioceses and regions. They are the venues for choral festivals raising the standards of music in the parishes and preserving a tradition of participation in an age when so much music is mechanical and consumerist.

In many places the cathedral is the only really large building suitable for the performance of great works, and so they find themselves acting as hosts for concerts put on by other bodies. Although the facilities do not necessarily rival those of a purpose built concert-hall, often the atmosphere is better, particularly for the performances of sacred music and it is significant that the London Festival Orchestra on tour through England and Scotland chooses to call its season 'Cathedral Classics' and deliberately to go only to cathedrals.

Perhaps more important than professional concerts, though, is the opportunity which cathedrals now give to local young people to perform great music in a noble setting. Through enlightened educational policies in schools, England is now teeming with talented young musicians, many of them from very modest and cramped homes. It is a joy to us in the cathedrals to offer them a rare chance to participate in transcendence and to be touched by greatness; and it is only right to record that some of our best experiences have been with the very young from primary schools and with music-making by the disabled or those from special schools with special educational needs.

Much of our concern is naturally with the preservation and transmission of our musical heritage from the past, but our tradition is an ever-flowing stream, with new works continually being commissioned and written. The organist at Rochester was a notable composer; some of my happiest moments as a priest were spent discussing texts with him, knowing that he had a rare gift of responding creatively to the right words. Like the Scandinavian churches, the Church of England has also benefited from a great upsurge in hymn writing in the last years, some of it of mediocre quality but the best very good indeed.

Other performing arts tend to take second place to music, but the medieval tradition of sacred drama (mystery plays and passion plays) has been revived – and new pieces are also being produced. The great turning point came with the commissioning by Dean George Bell of Canterbury of *Murder in the Cathedral* by T. S. Eliot shortly before the Second World War, but drama is now an accepted part of a cathedral's programme and dance is increasingly so.

Where the visual arts are concerned much of our effort and of our resources necessarily goes into the conservation of the glass, the sculpture, the wood work and the comparatively small amount of painting which is left to us. In recent years however there have been many new commissions and

even new art forms, like engraving on glass. Some of these
have been integral to the design of new cathedrals, of which
Coventry is the best known example. But new windows by
Marc Chagall, for instance, have been commissioned for the
ancient cathedrals of Chichester and Salisbury, new statues
for Llandaff and Salisbury and Rochester, a new tapestry for
Chichester and a set of new banners for Winchester. There
has been an unexpected renaissance in embroidery in England in the last decades, comparable to the unexpected
renaissance in hymnography. At a glance you can see the difference between conventional vestments from ecclesiastical
outfitters and the splendid new copes, in new materials and
new patterns, from the new generation of embroiderers.

Many of us long for the day when once again the church
will be a major patron of the arts; and once again people's
eyes will be informed by the expression in wood and stone,
in bronze and silk, of a truly Christian humanism. For the
moment, the financial means just do not lie to hand, and we
can only report isolated instances and the attempt of some
church people, at least, to stay in contact with creative artists
and craftsmen. Certainly I can bear witness that the single
most satisfying episode in my ministry as Dean of Rochester
was the time I spent discussing the incarnation with a sculp-
tor, preparing for us a statue of Mary and the Child Christ,
donated by a single generous benefactor and now giving plea-
sure to many who rejoice to see this representation of a
mother and child, and deepening the faith of those who see in
them the Son of God and the Mother of God.

What I enjoyed fleetingly at Rochester during a single
commission, some cathedrals, notably Durham, have enjoyed
more permanently by boldly – after the manner of universities with their writers-in-residence – employing an artist-in-
residence. The clergy speak of the enrichment and challenge,
which come to us and to our modes of perception from having an artist in our midst, and the artists of the inspiration
which comes from the cathedral – both as a building and as
a way of life.

For the greatest contribution cathedrals make to culture

is not the patronage or preservation of individual works of art. It is the living of life in a community, open to the world around it and sensitive to its needs, but deriving its rhythms and its values from elsewhere, so that it may continue to offer something new and challenging, healing and refreshing to the world and to the rest of the church. All the elements which sociologists tell us are necessary for community are there: space, time, folklore, symbols, shared memories and common purposes. These things make possible mutual care, reliable relationships and growth into personal maturity for the poor in spirit and them that mourn. And by making the major concerns of the age their own and conveying them to their dioceses, they can also encourage and succour those who hunger and thirst after righteousness. The cathedrals of England have developed a culture which goes some way to replacing what was lost in the life of the nation at the Dissolution of the Monasteries. In the so-called Dark Ages, Benedictine monasticism preserved what could be saved of the culture of Graeco-Roman antiquity and transmitted the Gospel to the new nations of northern Europe and to succeeding generations. In our age, which is also characterised by new energies and new forms of barbarism, the cathedrals have a unique role in civilising and evangelising Europe with the music of God's word of life.

7

Cathedrals and Society:
The Church's Relationship to the Nation

ROBERT JEFFERY
The Dean of Worcester

In 1943 the work to revise Cathedral statutes, that had been underway for seven years, was completed. In that year the then Editor of Crockford (Dean Malden of Wells, who was very given to Latin quotations) commented as follows:

> It is sometimes said that the present day is the Cathedral Age. It is true that there are more Cathedral Churches in England than ever before. Two new ones (one on an unprecedented scale) are under construction, and since this century began several parish churches have been raised to Cathedral rank, and have undergone, or are undergoing, extensive alterations to fit them for their new dignity. The ancient cathedrals are objects of more widespread interest than at any previous period; partly, perhaps, because until the recent restraint of motoring they were more accessible than they had ever been. It is, however, probably true that they are admired as architectural monuments more highly than they are appreciated as religious institutions. As the latter we believe them to have become of unique and supreme importance to the whole Church, as the principal repositories of the Anglican tradition of faith and worship in a cloudy and dark day. We do not, of course, imply that the Anglican Tradition is a *Summa Christinanitatis*; but we are quite sure that it is something which the

whole Christian world can by no means afford to lose, any more than civilisation can afford to lose the political ideas embodied in the British Empire.

Many might today question this last statement, for in retrospect many would see the Empire as an example of commercial exploitation, imperial domination and racial suppression, but the parallel is interesting and the picture he gives of cathedrals, in some way embodying the spirit of Anglicanism and of the nation, is the matter we need to examine and see what we can learn from it.

Within the ecclesiastical world there are two main national shrines, St Paul's Cathedral and Westminster Abbey, which typify this more than most. To such buildings Royalty go to be married, the nation turns in prayer at time of war and in thanksgiving at the end of war. In such buildings lie the great and good of the nation and those not buried there are often commemorated there in some way or other. Of those who saw it, who can forget Churchill's funeral at St Paul's Cathedral? In these buildings and at Windsor lie the centres of the great orders of honour in our society: the Orders of the British Empire, St Michael and St George, the Order of the Bath and of the Garter. Such buildings are almost an arm of the State. To them people turn for national celebrations. What do the shrines say? What do they embody?

Cathedrals come to embody the spirit of the state .They assist in perpetuating the myth and story of the nation. They become part of what holds the nation together. There are important questions to be raised about the nature of national cohesion and what happens when the accepted landmarks, like the monarchy, the judiciary, parliament, the church,the arts, the sense of national tradition, are for one reason or other brought into question. When one part is under question the rest tend to follow. We seem to be in such a position at the moment and, as a result, national cohesion becomes threatened and weakened. The argument can however be put the other way round. The cohesive nature of society may be strong when all accept a common faith and share a common heritage. But these days are now past. Ours is now a multicultural multi-faith society; we may need to look for cohesion elsewhere. Thus quite recently the political philosopher Dr John Grey has argued the reverse case. To give up the established church he says would be one way to achieve social cohesion. So he writes:

> Giving up the fiction that we are a Christian country has many potential benefits. Most importantly it recognises the reality of religious pluralism and takes one step towards building – or rebuilding – a common national culture.

This is an argument to ponder which in years to come might reveal itself in a multi-faith coronation and the use of cathedrals by other faiths. These are things which many would be unhappy about.

If, at present, St Paul's Cathedral and Westminster Abbey are at the heart of this process as national shrines every other cathedral is in some ways a reflection of it. In the county, in the city, each cathedral is a bridge between the sacred and the secular. National religion expresses itself on Remembrance Sunday or in special services for the emergency services or for those killed on the roads. They are places to which people turn for that symbolic act, which expresses the corporate mind and the corporate identity. Regimental flags are laid in Cathedral Military Chapels. All have their place. Civic services abound for the new Mayor. Regiments commemorate points in their history. Schools come at beginning and end of term. Universities use cathedrals for degree ceremonies. The Royal Maundy ceremonies move round the Cathedrals of the land. In all these ways Church and state become linked; cathedrals become sacramental of the inter-relationship.

But is it right? Is the Church simply affirming the role of the state whatever the state does? Is the church's function to consecrate the status quo? That is the underlying assumption of much that goes on and there is often a terrible row when that assumption is questioned: as when Archbishop Runcie refused to take a triumphalist line on the Falklands War, the Red Dean preached at Canterbury, or the Dean allowed

'Hair' to be performed in St Paul's Cathedral.

Cathedrals are subservient to the state in many ways. All Deans are appointed by the Crown, also many Canonries – in some cathedrals, all of them. The Church thus comes to be at the mercy of political patronage. In the middle of the nineteenth century the Dean of Worcester was the Prime Minister's brother and held at least one other living as well. There is always a risk that the state will exercise its patronage to ensure that the Church does indeed ratify the ways of government. There is a risk that ambitious clergy will pander to politicians in the hope of preferment.

We have to return to first principles. What is the Church for? What should be its relation to the state? What may be right in settled times may not work at times of turbulence and change.

Kierkegaard in his famous 'Attack on Christendom' in his very sharp way regards state religion as a contradiction in terms. By colluding with the state in any way Christianity was denying its very soul, so he writes of the state Church:

> For the sake of God in heaven and all that is holy, shun the priests, shun them, those abominable men whose livelihood is to prevent thee from so much as becoming aware of what Christianity is and who thereby would transform thee into what they understand by a true Christian, a paid member of the State church or national church or whatever they prefer to call it.

Fr Richard Benson put it more succinctly in the phrase, 'When Constantine took up the Cross the Church laid it down'.

The relationship of Church and state was put in a typically paradoxical manner by G.K. Chesterton in his hymn, 'O God of Earth and Altar':

> Bind in a living tether
> The Prince and priest and thrall,
> Bind all our lives together;
> Smite us and save us all.

There is enough in scripture and in history to make us be duly cautious of state religion. At the same time to shun it as Kierkegaard would is in great danger of producing an unincarnational faith unrelated to the world. Dr Alec Vidler in a famous essay in *Soundings* argued a strong case for preserving the Establishment which he summed up as follows:

> A national church is a standing witness to the fact that man, every man, is a twofold creature with a twofold allegiance, whether he realises it or not. He is a citizen of an earthly temporal state and as such has duties to perform and needs to be satisfied. But he is more than that. He has a mysterious origin and destiny and spiritual capacities for freedom and fullness of life which are not within the power or control of civil government. A man is not only a political creature, but also a spiritual being who belongs to a realm of eternal values which lifts him above all the realms of this world even when he is immersed in them. A national church, recognised as such by the state, is a constant, public and impressive reminder of this fact.

Such a view may now seem a little dated. As the state becomes more and more secular, its acknowledgement of humanity's need for spiritual realities, seems very vapid. At the same time, that very fact means that a national church has an even greater responsibility to remind the nation of the spiritualities. Cathedrals are ideally placed to be the base for this function.

Given that there is still a residual interconnection between Church and state, we then have to pose the question about how the Church should react to this situation. The Church has historically, at many times, developed three different attitudes. One approach is that of total rejection of the state by the Church. This turns the church into a ghetto. It is the path of introversion which cathedrals are very tempted to follow, as I mentioned earlier.

If rejection is a negative option, then total acceptance of the state is equally so. For to allow the sate to determine the Gospel preached is to surrender the challenge, the judgmental and cutting edge of the Gospel. To allow the state to take over becomes a denial of the Kingdom. This too has happened to the Church from time to time and has shown itself in surrendering to state patronage for the sake of preferment, offering a non-challenging gospel which is one of comfort. It is revealed in what has been called 'The Comfortable Pew' and the 'Suburban Captivity of the Churches',

But there is a third way which has been variously called 'critical involvement' or 'critical solidarity'. Here the Church accepts the interaction of Church and state and uses it to engage with the fundamental issues of society and life. Such a view requires an openness to the world and a willingness to engage in the world around us. It has been wisely said by Dr Margaret Kane that 'the inevitable consequence of a view of mission which does not take seriously the Church's role in reshaping society must be that the Church will itself be shaped by society'. Indeed, an interaction is inevitable.

It has to be said that in some ways a cathedral is not the ideal platform for this task. For these massive buildings which on the one side speak of humanity's aspirations, also speak of power, dominance and a view of the world where the Church dominates and rules. There is therefore a major task in not allowing the old views of the world, of which the walls of cathedrals speak, to remain dominant today for if they do, we will not be heard.

There are subtle matters of judgement here. How and where does the Gospel impinge?. We need to be very alert. The new report of the Archbishops' Commission on Cathedrals has already been criticised as being too commercially driven. Accountants are in danger of calling the tune. There is a great difference between running a cathedral efficiently and deliberately running a cathedral to make a profit and draw its income primarily from its visitors. No, we have to be clear about our ultimate vision and aim. The aim of a cathedral cannot be chiefly to be well marketed or to make a profit and keep in the black, desirable as all these may be. The primary aim of the cathedral must be to worship God and make the Gospel known, whatever the price. We dare not be diverted to other ends even for the sake of survival(for does not the Gospel call us to lose our lives?).

A current commercial term is to prepare a 'Mission statement', but in relation to the role of the Church in Society a Mission statement can be a primary task in every sense of the meaning of Mission. Producing a Mission statement has been a task which we have recently completed at Worcester. It was prepared after considerable consultation and drawn up by lay people in the congregation. The final version reads:

WORCESTER CATHEDRAL
MISSION STATEMENT

For over 1,300 years, a building dedicated to the service of God has stood on the site of Worcester Cathedral.

The present building, started over 900 years ago by Bishop Wulfstan, stands in a changing world as an inspiration and as a reminder of the constancy of God's love.

We, the clergy, lay staff, volunteers and regular worshippers here form a community and have a common purpose: to proclaim the glory of God and to bear witness to Christ's loving presence in the world.

We seek to carry out this mission by:

— maintaining the daily round of worship as part of the living church and by seeking continually to enhance and develop the pattern of services in this great Cathedral.

— working together in a ministry of welcome and hospitality to all who come to the Cathedral, so that the building and its people do offer a welcome as Christ does to all who come to Him.

— caring for this great building and preserving its unique ability to allow space for anonymity, to provide solace and to provoke wonder.

— recognising the Cathedral's potential to build bridges in a divided world and to bring together the sacred and the secular, the rich and the poor, people of all faiths and none.

— promoting the use of the Cathedral as a focus for artistic and other creative activities within the City and Diocese.

— advancing scholarship and learning, so that the understanding of God's work and purpose in the world may be increased.

— involving parishes and Diocesan organisations in wel-

come, hospitality, worship and education in the Cathedral.
— encouraging young people to visit the Cathedral and to
join in its activities, thereby influencing our thinking and
helping us to stay in touch with the world around us.

It is this document which will now become the basis of
a ten-year plan which we have just started preparing.

Such a process will inevitably lead us into an engage-
ment of critical involvement in the world around us. If there
are great national shrines like St Paul's Cathedral and Westminster Abbey, then cathedrals can and should be seen as
regional shrines with regional roles. The centralising ten-
dency of government over the last fifteen years has been to
the detriment of local identity and local initiative. I find it
strange that in the context of Europe a government which is
committed to a principle of subsidiarity refuses to apply the
same principle to regional and local government. I am
increasingly convinced that the growth of violence and crime
in our society is directly related to an almost deliberate pol-
icy of devaluing people. The centralisation of powers means
that people feel little local commitment. The encouragement
of people to engage in trivia like a large number of TV channels, cheap and repetitive music, the commercialisation of
almost every aspect of life, the treating of people as units in
the market and the encouragement of greed through things
like the National Lottery, in fact, devalues people and makes
them feel of little or no significance .The loss of local identity,
the universalisation of culture, all removes real meaning from
people. The result is frustration, violence, addiction and mis-
ery. The critical solidarity of the Church thus can begin
through a Cathedral ministry which reminds people of their
roots, reminds them of their history and local identity. A ministry which identifies and addresses local issues and regional
concerns, which uses every opportunity to revalue life and
give meaning and identity to people is a vital task. A cathedral, just because it is regional rather than local, has opportunities to engage in that task more fully than most. It is a
task which should not be ignored. A cathedral has a flexibility about it which enables it to relate to the intermediate lev-

els in society: County Councils, Regional Health Authorities, Chambers of Commerce, Universities, Planning Authorities, Regional Broadcasting and Press can all identify with a Cathedral and vice versa. Thus it is that cathedrals are ideally situated to be centres of Christian apologetic applying the Christian Gospel, the Christian understanding of Human nature and ethical standards to regional life. So again we see the cathedral as one of the institutions which give cohesion to regional life.

Cathedrals also have often provided an ideal platform for the Christian prophet – clergy with a commitment to specific issues . Cathedral appointments need to be used not simply to carry on the life of the Cathedral but to provide a platform for those whose hearts and minds are burning with passion for Christian apologetic, making connections, building bridges. Alongside that can go the quiet dialogue, the pastoral care of people who often bear the burden of political or public office and who rarely find an understanding ear or a supporting arm. Such people tend to be drawn to cathedral life and there is a real ministry here.

CONCLUSION

So we come to the end of this series of papers which I hope have given you some insights into the complexities and opportunities of Cathedral Life and ministry. The *Crockford* editor, Dean Malden, often reflected on cathedrals. In 1929 he commented on the changes at the Reformation with these words:

> For sometime after the Reformation men may well have been in some perplexity as to the use to which these institutions could be put when the saying of masses for the souls of founders and benefactors could no longer be their principal occupation. It is however clear that in our world Cathedral churches have at least three functions of the highest importance to discharge as Homes of Study, Schools of Sacred Music, and Exemplars of dignity and beauty in worship.

This principle still stands, but it would be the view of this generation that they are also centres of Mission and Bridges between Church and state. But at another level, cathedrals are simply a macrocosm of what every church and congregation should be seeking in its own area and life. For fundamentally the Christian vocation of us all is the same, to take up the Cross and follow him who is the light and the hope of all the world.